BOLSTERING THE GOVERNMENT'S CYBERSECURITY: ASSESSING THE RISK OF KASPERSKY LAB PRODUCTS TO THE FEDERAL GOVERNMENT

HEARING

BEFORE THE

SUBCOMMITTEE ON OVERSIGHT &

COMMITTEE ON SCIENCE, SPACE, AND TECHNOLOGY

HOUSE OF REPRESENTATIVES

ONE HUNDRED FIFTEENTH CONGRESS

FIRST SESSION

October 25, 2017

Serial No. 115–33

Printed for the use of the Committee on Science, Space, and Technology

Available via the World Wide Web: http://science.house.gov

U.S. GOVERNMENT PUBLISHING OFFICE

27–672PDF   WASHINGTON : 2018

COMMITTEE ON SCIENCE, SPACE, AND TECHNOLOGY

HON. LAMAR S. SMITH, Texas, *Chair*

FRANK D. LUCAS, Oklahoma
DANA ROHRABACHER, California
MO BROOKS, Alabama
RANDY HULTGREN, Illinois
BILL POSEY, Florida
THOMAS MASSIE, Kentucky
JIM BRIDENSTINE, Oklahoma
RANDY K. WEBER, Texas
STEPHEN KNIGHT, California
BRIAN BABIN, Texas BARBARA
COMSTOCK, Virginia
GARY PALMER, Alabama
BARRY LOUDERMILK, Georgia
RALPH LEE ABRAHAM, Louisiana
DRAIN LaHOOD, Illinois
DANIEL WEBSTER, Florida
JIM BANKS, Indiana
ANDY BIGGS, Arizona
ROGER W. MARSHALL, Kansas
NEAL P. DUNN, Florida
CLAY HIGGINS, Louisiana

EDDIE BERNICE JOHNSON, Texas
ZOE LOFGREN, California
DANIEL LIPINSKI, Illinois
SUZANNE BONAMICI, Oregon
ALAN GRAYSON, Florida
AMI BERA, California
ELIZABETH H. ESTY, Connecticut
MARC A. VEASEY, Texas
DONALD S. BEYER, JR., Virginia
JACKY ROSEN, Nevada
JERRY MCNERNEY, California
ED PERLMUTTER, Colorado
PAUL TONKO, New York
BILL FOSTER, Illinois
MARK TAKANO, California
COLLEEN HANABUSA, Hawaii
CHARLIE CRIST, Florida

CONTENTS

October 25, 2017

IV

BOLSTERING THE GOVERNMENT'S CYBERSECURITY: ASSESSING THE RISK OF KASPERSKY LAB PRODUCTS TO THE FEDERAL GOVERNMENT

Wednesday, October 25, 2017

House of Representatives,
Subcommittee on Oversight and
Committee on Science, Space, and Technology,
Washington, D.C.

The Subcommittee met, pursuant to call, at 10:06 a.m., in Room 2318 of the Rayburn House Office Building, Hon. Darin LaHood [Chairman of the Subcommittee] presiding.

LAMAR S. SMITH, Texas
CHAIRMAN

EDDIE BERNICE JOHNSON, Texas
RANKING MEMBER

Congress of the United States
House of Representatives

COMMITTEE ON SCIENCE, SPACE, AND TECHNOLOGY

2321 RAYBURN HOUSE OFFICE BUILDING

WASHINGTON, DC 20515–6301

(202) 225–6371
www.science.house.gov

Subcommittee on Oversight

Bolstering the Government's Cybersecurity: Assessing the Risk of Kaspersky Lab Products to the Federal Government

Wednesday, October 25
10:00 a.m.
2318 Rayburn House Office Building

Witnesses

Ms. Donna Dodson, Associate Director and Chief Cybersecurity Advisor, Information Technology Laboratory; and Chief Cybersecurity Advisor, National Institute of Standards and Technology

Mr. David Shive, Chief Information Officer, U.S. General Services Administration

Mr. James Norton, President, Play-Action Strategies LLC; and Adjunct Professor, Johns Hopkins University

Mr. Sean Kanuck, Director of Future Conflict and Cyber Security, International Institute for Strategic Studies

U.S. HOUSE OF REPRESENTATIVES
COMMITTEE ON SCIENCE, SPACE, AND TECHNOLOGY

HEARING CHARTER

October 19, 2017

TO: Members, Subcommittee on Oversight

FROM: Majority Staff, Committee on Science, Space, and Technology

SUBJECT: Oversight Subcommittee hearing: *Bolstering the Government's Cybersecurity: Assessing the Risk of Kaspersky Lab Products to the Federal Government*

The Subcommittee on Oversight will hold a hearing titled *Bolstering the Government's Cybersecurity: Assessing the Risk of Kaspersky Lab Products to the Federal Government* on Wednesday, October 25, 2017, at 10:00 a.m. in Room 2318 of the Rayburn House Office Building.

Hearing Purpose:

The purpose of this hearing is to examine the concerns raised regarding the risks associated with utilizing Kaspersky Lab products on federal government information technology systems ("IT systems") and the federal government's response to the concerns. Witnesses will discuss the government's cybersecurity posture, potential cybersecurity risks Kaspersky Lab's products pose to agency IT systems, and ways to improve agency practices related to design, acquisition, development, modernization, use and performance of federal IT resources.

Witness List:

- **Ms. Donna Dodson**, Associate Director and Chief Cybersecurity Advisor, Information Technology Laboratory; and Chief Cybersecurity Advisor, National Institute of Standards and Technology
- **Mr. David Shive**, Chief Information Officer, U.S. General Services Administration
- **Mr. James Norton**, President, Play-Action Strategies LLC; and Adjunct Professor, Johns Hopkins University
- **Mr. Sean Kanuck**, Director of Future Conflict and Cyber Security, International Institute for Strategic Studies

Staff Contact:

For questions related to the hearing, please contact Drew Colliatie or Tom Connally of the Majority Staff at 202-225-6371.

Chairman LAHOOD. The Subcommittee on Oversight will come to order.

Without objection, the Chair is authorized to declare recesses of the Subcommittee at any time.

I want to welcome you to today's hearing titled "Bolstering the Government's Cybersecurity: Assessing the Risk of Kaspersky Lab Products to the Federal Government."

The subject of today's hearing involves some information that is classified. I remind Members that their questions may call for a response that the witnesses know to be classified. Please be mindful of this fact. I would like to instruct the witnesses to answer to the best of their ability, but should an answer call for sensitive information, it may be addressed if we vote to move into executive session at the end of the hearing.

At this time, I'm going to yield to the Chairman of the Full Committee, Chairman Lamar Smith, for his opening statement at this time.

Chairman SMITH. Thank you, Mr. Chairman. I appreciate your deferring to me and yielding me time, and let me apologize to the panelists. I have to leave immediately for a Judiciary Committee markup where they are considering a piece of legislation that I've introduced, so that's why I have to leave early, but perhaps I'll be able to get back.

Cybersecurity breaches are so prevalent today that it is hard to keep track of them. Every news cycle seems to include a new major incident. To address the federal government's cybersecurity weaknesses, the Committee hopes to bring H.R. 1224, the NIST Cybersecurity Framework, Assessment, and Auditing Act of 2017, to the House Floor for a vote.

Specific to Kaspersky Lab, new revelations regarding cyber-espionage continue to surface. This Committee has engaged in robust oversight of Kaspersky Lab, thanks to questions raised by Congressman Higgins during a hearing in June.

On July 27, 2017, this Committee requested all federal departments and agencies to disclose their use of Kaspersky Lab products. This was less than a month after the U.S. General Services Administration banned Kaspersky Lab products from its government-wide schedule contracts. However, we still have questions: Why was the software approved for government use? And was removing it from the approved GSA schedule sufficient to protect U.S. interests?

I support this Administration's subsequent actions. The interagency working group on cybersecurity has begun to address the problem.

On September 13, 2017, the Department of Homeland Security issued a government-wide order directing federal departments and agencies to identify and remove the company's products from use. In subsequent hearings, we will need to assess whether the federal government's response has been sufficient.

While once considered reputable, Kaspersky Lab, its founder and their Russian ties have created a significant risk to U.S. security. According to several media investigations, these connections have allowed Kaspersky Lab to be exploited not only by the Russian government but also by criminal hackers around the world. Mr.

Kaspersky's history and recent remarks have done little to alleviate these concerns.

As we move forward with this hearing and future hearings, we expect to uncover all aspects of Kaspersky Lab. We are particularly interested in what led the previous Administration to include Kaspersky Lab products on two GSA schedules. I look forward to the testimony of Mr. Shive, the GSA Chief Administration and Information Officer. I am also interested in proactive steps GSA has taken to assist other departments and agencies in rooting out the presence of Kaspersky products on their systems.

Also, we need to better understand the recent news related to the breach of an NSA contractor's personal computer.

The threat Kaspersky Lab products present to the government has now been publicly identified and confirmed by the Israeli government. I urge anyone with knowledge of potential risks to contact the Committee and share that information with us. We must be vigilant in addressing this wolf in sheep's clothing.

Thank you, Mr. Chairman. I'll yield back.

[The prepared statement of Chairman Smith follows:]

For Immediate Release
October 25, 2017

Media Contacts: Thea McDonald, Brandon VerVelde
(202) 225-6371

Statement from Chairman Lamar Smith (R-Texas)

Bolstering the Government's Cybersecurity: Assessing the Risk of Kaspersky Lab Products to the Federal Government

Chairman Smith: Cybersecurity breaches are so prevalent today that it is hard to keep track of them. Every news cycle seems to include a new major incident.

To address the federal government's cybersecurity weaknesses, the Committee hopes to bring H.R. 1224, the NIST Cybersecurity Framework, Assessment, and Auditing Act of 2017, to the House floor for a vote.

Specific to Kaspersky Lab, new revelations regarding cyber-espionage continue to surface. This Committee has engaged in robust oversight of Kaspersky Lab, thanks to questions raised by Congressman Higgins during a hearing in June.

On July 27, 2017, this Committee requested all federal departments and agencies to disclose their use of Kaspersky Lab products.

This was less than a month after the U.S. General Services Administration (GSA) banned Kaspersky Lab products from its government-wide schedule contracts. However, we still have questions: Why was the software approved for government use? And was removing it from the approved GSA schedule sufficient to protect US interests?

I support this administration's subsequent actions. The interagency working group on cybersecurity has begun to address the problem.

On September 13, 2017, the Department of Homeland Security issued a government-wide order directing federal departments and agencies to identify and remove the company's products from use. In subsequent hearings, we will need to assess whether the federal government's response has been sufficient.

While once considered reputable, Kaspersky Lab, its founder and their Russian ties have created a significant risk to U.S. security. According to several media investigations, these connections have allowed Kaspersky Lab to be exploited not only by the Russian government but also by criminal hackers around the world.

Mr. Kaspersky's history and recent remarks have done little to alleviate these concerns.

As we move forward with this hearing and future hearings, we expect to uncover all aspects of Kaspersky Lab.

We are particularly interested in what led the previous administration to include Kaspersky Lab products on two GSA schedules. I look forward to the testimony of Mr. Shive, the GSA Chief Information Officer.

I am also interested in proactive steps GSA has taken to assist other departments and agencies in rooting out the presence of Kaspersky products on their systems.

Also, we need to better understand the recent news related to the breach of an NSA contractor's personal computer.

The threat Kaspersky Lab products present to the government has now been publicly identified and confirmed by the Israeli government.

I urge anyone with knowledge of potential risks to contact the Committee and share that information with us. We must be vigilant in addressing this wolf in sheep's clothing.

###

Chairman LAHOOD. Thank you, Mr. Chairman.

At this time I recognize myself for five minutes for an opening statement, and again I want to welcome our witnesses here today.

Today we intend to discuss and evaluate the cybersecurity posture of the federal government. Specifically, we will examine the concerns that this Committee has raised about the risks associated with using Kaspersky Lab's products on federal information technology systems, as well as actions that the Trump Administration has taken in response to these concerns.

As part of today's hearing, we will hear from government and private sector cybersecurity experts about the potential risks that Kaspersky Lab products and services pose to agency IT systems. In doing so, we hope to find effective and efficient ways to improve agency practices related to the design, acquisition, development, modernization, use and performance of federal IT resources.

Kaspersky Lab is based in Moscow, Russia, and was founded in 1997 by Eugene Kaspersky. The company is one of the world's largest providers of cybersecurity software and services, including both consumer and enterprise solutions. As early as 2015, reports began to surface alleging that Mr. Kaspersky maintained close ties to Russian spies. Not only for Mr. Kaspersky—not only was Mr. Kaspersky educated at a KGB-sponsored university, he also wrote code for the Soviet military.

In May of this year, the concerns surrounding Kaspersky Lab were brought to public light during a Senate Intelligence Committee hearing, where several intelligence community officials unanimously affirmed they would be uncomfortable using Kaspersky Lab's software and services. In June of this year, during this Committee's hearing on the WannaCry ransomware outbreak, our witnesses expressed similar concerns.

The matter reached a tipping point in July, when the General Services Administration, the GSA, announced the removal of Kaspersky Lab products from its preapproved government contracts schedules.

On July 27, the Committee commenced its investigation of the matter, with Chairman Smith probing 22 federal departments and agencies on their use of Kaspersky Lab products and services. Last month, the Trump Administration took another step toward addressing the concerns surrounding Kaspersky when the Department of Homeland Security issued Binding Operational Directive 17–01, ordering all federal departments and agencies to remove Kaspersky Lab software from their systems within 90 days.

Mr. Kaspersky has been highly critical of the U.S. throughout this entire process, frequently arguing that no public evidence existed to support the concerns raised about his company. Earlier this month, however, several prominent American news organizations published startling revelations that confirmed this Committee's gravest concerns: the Russian government has wielded Kaspersky's software as a tool for cyber-espionage. This Administration has been proactively remedying the Kaspersky situation, and we must continue to take steps to ensure that we do not repeat past mistakes.

To that end, I look forward to hearing from our expert witnesses about how Kaspersky became approved for use on federal systems, the policies and procedures that can be implemented to bolster the federal government's cybersecurity risk-management processes, and the actions that must be taken to ensure that federal systems remain secure against nefarious cyber actors.

Thank you.

[The prepared statement of Chairman LaHood follows:]

For Immediate Release
October 25, 2017

Media Contacts: Thea McDonald, Brandon VerVelde
(202) 225-6371

Statement from Chairman Darin LaHood (R-Ill.)

Bolstering the Government's Cybersecurity: Assessing the Risk of Kaspersky Lab Products to the Federal Government

Chairman LaHood: Good morning and welcome to today's Oversight Subcommittee hearing, "Bolstering the Government's Cybersecurity: Assessing the Risk of Kaspersky Lab Products to the Federal Government."

Today we intend to discuss and evaluate the cybersecurity posture of the federal government. Specifically, we will examine the concerns that this Committee has raised about the risks associated with using Kaspersky Lab's products on federal information technology (IT) systems, as well as actions that the Trump administration has taken in response to these concerns.

As part of today's hearing, we will hear from government and private sector cybersecurity experts about the potential risks that Kaspersky Lab products and services pose to agency IT systems. In doing so, we hope to find effective and efficient ways to improve agency practices related to the design, acquisition, development, modernization, use and performance of federal IT resources.

Kaspersky Lab is based in Moscow, Russia, and was founded in 1997 by Eugene Kaspersky. The company is one of the world's largest providers of cybersecurity software and services, including both consumer and enterprise solutions.

As early as 2015, reports began to surface alleging that Mr. Kaspersky maintained close ties to Russian spies. Not only was Mr. Kaspersky educated at a KGB-sponsored university, he also wrote code for the Soviet military.

In May of this year, the concerns surrounding Kaspersky Lab were brought to public light during a Senate Intelligence Committee hearing, where several intelligence community officials unanimously affirmed they would be uncomfortable using Kaspersky Lab's software and services. In June of this year, during this Committee's hearing on the WannaCry ransomware outbreak, our witnesses expressed similar concerns. The matter reached a tipping point in July, when the General Services Administration (GSA) announced the removal of Kaspersky Lab products from its pre-approved government contracts schedules.

On July 27, the Committee commenced its investigation of the matter, with Chairman Smith probing 22 federal departments and agencies on their use of Kaspersky Lab products and services.

Last month, the Trump administration took another step toward addressing the concerns surrounding Kaspersky when the Department of Homeland Security (DHS) issued Binding Operational Directive (BOD) 17-01, ordering all federal departments and agencies to remove Kaspersky Lab software from their systems within 90 days.

Mr. Kaspersky has been highly critical of the U.S. throughout this entire process, frequently arguing that no public evidence existed to support the concerns raised about his company.

Earlier this month, however, several prominent American news organizations published startling revelations that confirmed this Committee's gravest concerns: the Russian government has wielded Kaspersky's software as a tool for cyber-espionage.

This administration has been proactively remedying the Kaspersky situation. And we must continue to take steps to ensure that we do not repeat past mistakes.

To that end, I look forward to hearing from our expert witnesses about how Kaspersky became approved for use on federal systems, the policies and procedures that can be implemented to bolster the federal government's cybersecurity risk-management processes, and the actions that must be taken to ensure that federal systems remain secure against nefarious cyber actors.

###

Chairman LaHood. At this time I now recognize the Ranking Member, the gentleman from Virginia, for his opening statement.

Mr. Beyer. Thank you, Chairman LaHood, and thank all of you for being with us.

Security concerns related to the Kaspersky Lab products and reported ties between Eugene Kaspersky, his company, and Russian intelligence services have been brewing within the U.S. intelligence community for years. This is deeply troubling given that Kaspersky Lab, whose main product is antivirus software, has offices in 32 countries, approximately 270,000 corporate clients, and its software is used by approximately 400 million people worldwide. And, until just recently, the U.S. Government also used KL software.

The founder of Kaspersky Lab, Eugene Kaspersky, is a software engineer educated at a KGB cryptography institute who also worked for the Russian intelligence services before starting his software company in 1997. He's been described as the Bill Gates of Russia. Despite his background and the concerns of the U.S. intelligence community, the company has vigorously argued that it has no ties to any government.

Concerns about connections between Kaspersky Lab and Russian intelligence services have become more pronounced over the last year. In April, the Senate Intelligence Committee asked the Director of National Intelligence and the U.S. Attorney General to look into Kaspersky employees' potential ties with Russian intelligence. In May, six U.S. intelligence agency directors, including the Directors of the CIA and NSA, told the Intelligence Committee that they would not be comfortable using Kaspersky products on their networks. In June, it was reported that FBI agents had interviewed U.S.-based employees of Kaspersky Lab, and in July, Bloomberg Businessweek published a story referencing internal company emails that showed a close working relationship between Kaspersky Lab and Russian intelligence.

Finally, earlier this month, the New York Times reported that Israeli intelligence were able to determine that Russian government hackers have been using the company's software to search for the code names of U.S. intelligence programs. Specifically, the Israelis discovered that a contractor to the National Security Agency had his data compromised over two years ago by these Russian hackers after he improperly took classified documents home and stored them on his home computer. Kaspersky's antivirus software had been installed on the contractor's home computer, and KL Lab has repeatedly denied any affiliation with the Russian hacking, but just today, the company admitted in a blog post that it had collected the NSA files through routine malware data collection.

All of this has led to legitimate security concerns about the use of Kaspersky Lab software. I am glad that the U.S. Government has realized this. In July, as our Chairman has said, the General Services Administration removed Kaspersky Lab from its list of approved federal vendors, and, last month, the Department of Homeland Security issued a Binding Operational Directive banning federal agencies from using any product or service offered by KL, giving federal agencies until mid-December to implement that directive.

But cybersecurity is no longer simply about defending our data from theft. It's also about defending our democracy from disinformation campaigns that combine cyber assaults with influence operations. Since the 2016 election, it has been well-established that Russia has spread falsehoods and disinformation, seeking to sow divisions between us and confusion among us. This is not, and should not be, a partisan issue. Together we should be striving to defend our democracy against those who seek to damage it.

Mr. Chairman, I hope we can have a future hearing where we hear from social scientists, researchers, and technical experts about the tools and technologies we can employ to help identify these evolving threats beyond traditional cybersecurity and defend against them.

I look forward to hearing from all our witnesses today and especially Sean Kanuck, who happens to be one of my constituents, an expert on these topics. He was appointed the first National Intelligence Officer for Cyber Issues in 2011 and served in that position at the National Security Council until 2016. Prior to that he spent ten years at the CIA in their Information Operations Center. Today he joins us as the Director of Future Conflict and Cyber Security at the International Institute for Strategic Studies. So Sean, welcome, and I look forward to all of your testimony.

Mr. Chairman, I yield back.

[The prepared statement of Mr. Beyer follows:]

<u>OPENING STATEMENT</u>
Ranking Member Don Beyer (D-VA)
of the Subcommittee on Oversight

House Committee on Science, Space and Technology
"Bolstering the Government's Cybersecurity:
Assessing the Risk of Kaspersky Lab Products to the Federal Government"
October 25, 2017

Thank you, Chairman LaHood.

Security concerns related to Kaspersky Lab products and reported ties between Eugene Kaspersky, his company, and Russian intelligence services have been brewing within the U.S. intelligence community for years. This is deeply troubling given that Kaspersky Lab – whose main product is anti-virus software – has offices in 32 countries, an estimated 270,000 corporate clients, and its software is used by approximately 400 million people worldwide. And, until just recently, the U.S. Government also used Kaspersky Lab's software.

The founder of Kaspersky Lab, Eugene Kaspersky, is a software engineer educated at a KGB cryptography institute who also worked for the Russian intelligence service before starting his software company in 1997. Eugene Kaspersky has been described as the "Bill Gates of Russia". Despite his background and the concerns of the U.S. intelligence community, the company has vigorously argued that it has no ties to any government.

Concerns about connections between Kaspersky Lab and Russian intelligence services have become more pronounced over the past year:
- In April, the Senate Intelligence Committee asked the Director of National Intelligence and U.S. Attorney General to look into Kaspersky employees' potential ties with Russian intelligence.
- In May, six U.S. intelligence agency directors, including the Directors of the CIA and NSA, told the Intelligence Committee that they would not be comfortable using Kaspersky products on their networks.
- In June, it was reported that FBI agents had interviewed U.S.-based employees of Kaspersky Lab.
- In July, Bloomberg Businessweek published a story referencing internal company emails that showed a close working relationship between Kaspersky Lab and Russian intelligence.

Finally, earlier this month, the New York Times reported that Israeli intelligence were able to determine that Russian government hackers have been using the company's software to search for the code names of U.S. intelligence programs. Specifically, the Israelis discovered that a contractor to the National Security Agency (NSA) had his data compromised over two years ago by these Russian hackers after he improperly took classified documents home and stored them on his home computer. Kaspersky's antivirus software had been installed on this contractor's home computer. Kaspersky Lab has repeatedly denied any affiliation with the Russian hacking, but just today, the company admitted in a blog post that it had collected the NSA files through routine malware data collection.

All of this has led to legitimate security concerns about the use of Kaspersky Lab software. I am glad that the U.S. Government has realized this: in July, the General Services Administration (GSA) removed Kaspersky Lab from its list of approved federal vendors. And, last month, the Department of Homeland Security (DHS) issued a Binding Operational Directive (BOD) banning federal agencies from using any product or service offered by Kaspersky Lab, giving federal agencies until mid-December to implement that directive.

But, cybersecurity is no longer simply about defending our data from theft. It is also about defending our democracy from disinformation campaigns that combine cyber assaults with influence operations. Since the 2016 election, it has been well-established that Russia has spread falsehoods and disinformation, seeking to sow divisions between us and confusion among us.

This is not, and should not be, a partisan issue – together we should be striving to defend our democracy against those who seek to damage it.

Mr. Chairman, I hope we can also have a future hearing where we hear from social scientists, researchers, and technical experts about the tools and technologies we can employ to help identify these evolving threats – beyond traditional cybersecurity – and defend against them. I hope that you will commit to that.

I look forward to hearing from all of our witnesses today and especially Sean Kanuck, who happens to be one of my constituents, and who is an expert on these topics. Mr. Kanuck was appointed the first National Intelligence Officer (NIO) for Cyber Issues in 2011 and served in that position at the National Security Council (NSC) until 2016. Prior to that he spent ten years at the Central Intelligence Agency's (CIA's) Information Operations Center. Today he joins us as the Director of Future Conflict and Cyber Security at the International Institute for Strategic Studies (IISS). Welcome Sean, and welcome to all of our witnesses.

Chairman LaHood. Thank you, Mr. Beyer.

At this time I now recognize the Ranking Member of the Full Committee, Ms. Johnson, for her opening statement.

Ms. Johnson. Thank you very much, Mr. Chairman.

Kaspersky Lab is one of the world's largest cybersecurity companies, and makes a popular antivirus program used by 400 million users worldwide. But recent concerns by the U.S. intelligence community about close connections between Kaspersky Lab, its founder Eugene Kaspersky, and the Russian intelligence services have led to much greater scrutiny of its activities.

This hearing is premised on examining what threat that Kaspersky software poses to the federal government. However, the federal government has already preemptively addressed that threat.

Last month, the Department of Homeland Security issued a directive that required all federal agencies to identify any of their networks using Kaspersky Lab software, and gave those agencies a 90-day deadline to initiate a plan to remove the Kaspersky Lab software from those computer systems. DHS decided that the security risk of having a Russian company embedded on federal computer networks was simply not worth it. I have confidence in the ability of the federal government agencies to eliminate the Kaspersky Lab products from their respective computer systems.

I am less confident, though, in our collective ability to identify and guard against cyber warfare actions from Russian state actors. Russian hackers have infiltrated some of our nation's nuclear power plants, private email accounts, and state election databases. Russia, according to a publicly available Intelligence Community assessment, conducted an influence campaign in 2016 to undermine public faith in the U.S. democratic process and to harm the campaign chances of Hillary Clinton winning the Presidency.

The intelligence assessment should be a wake-up call for all of us. We should expect attempts by foreign actors to affect future elections using computer hacking, social media, and other means, as was done in 2016.

Mr. Chairman, prior to the 2016 election, this Committee held a hearing to review guidelines for protecting voting and election systems including voter registration databases and voter machines. I believe a follow-up hearing would be appropriate to discuss protecting these same systems, in light of last year's events, as well as examining the sophisticated influence operations conducted by Russian intelligence services to disrupt our democratic processes and damage our democracy. With the knowledge of Russian cyber warfare actions in 2016, we can have a more robust discussion on the measures hostile actors have been using against America's voting infrastructure, and we can discuss measures that need to be taken to bolster the security of our elections.

Mr. Chairman, I hope that you seriously consider holding a 2016 election security postmortem with a focus on what the Science Committee can do to help protect the vote going forward.

I thank you, and yield back the balance of my time.

[The prepared statement of Ms. Johnson follows:]

<u>OPENING STATEMENT</u>
Ranking Member Eddie Bernice Johnson (D-TX)

House Committee on Science, Space, and Technology
Subcommittee on Oversight
*"Bolstering the Government's Cybersecurity: Assessing the Risk of Kaspersky Lab Products to the
Federal Government"*
October 25, 2017

Thank you Chairman LaHood. Kaspersky Lab is one of the world's largest cybersecurity companies, and makes a popular anti-virus program used by 400 million users worldwide. But recent concerns by the U.S. intelligence community about close connections between Kaspersky Lab, its founder Eugene Kaspersky, and the Russian Intelligence Services have led to much greater scrutiny of its activities. This hearing is premised on examining what threat Kaspersky software poses to the federal government. However, the federal government has already pre-emptively addressed that threat. Last month, the Department of Homeland Security (DHS) issued a directive that required all federal agencies to identify any of their networks using Kaspersky Lab software, and gave those agencies a 90-day deadline to initiate a plan to remove Kaspersky Lab software from those computer systems. DHS decided that the security risk of having a Russian company embedded on federal computer networks was simply not worth it.

I have confidence in the ability of federal government agencies to eliminate Kaspersky Lab products from their respective computer systems. I am less confident, though, in our collective ability to identify and guard against cyber warfare actions from Russian state actors. Russian hackers have infiltrated some of our nation's nuclear power plants, private e-mail accounts, and state election databases. Russia, according to a publicly available Intelligence Community assessment, conducted an influence campaign in 2016 to undermine public faith in the US democratic process and to harm Hillary Clinton's chances of winning the Presidency. That intelligence assessment should be a wake-up call for all of us. We should expect attempts by foreign actors to affect future elections, using computer hacking, social media, and other means, as was done in 2016.

Mr. Chairman, prior to the 2016 Election, this Committee held a hearing to review the guidelines for protecting voting and election systems—including voter registration databases and voting machines. I believe a follow-up hearing would be appropriate to discuss protecting these same systems, in the light of last year's events, as well as examining the sophisticated influence operations conducted by Russian intelligence services to disrupt our democratic processes and damage our democracy. With the knowledge of Russian cyber warfare actions in 2016, we can have a more robust discussion on the measures hostile actors have been using against America's voting infrastructure, and we can discuss measures that need to be taken to bolster the security of our elections.

Mr. Chairman, I hope that you seriously consider holding a 2016 election security postmortem, with a focus on what the Science Committee can do to help protect the vote going forward. Thank you and I yield back the balance of my remaining time.

Chairman LaHood. Thank you, Ms. Johnson.

At this time let me introduce our witnesses here today. Our first witness today is Ms. Donna Dodson, Associate Director and Chief Cybersecurity Advisor of the Information Technology Laboratory, and Chief Cybersecurity Advisor at the National Institute of Standards and Technology (NIST). Ms. Dodson began her career at NIST in 1987 as a Computer Science Researcher. In 2010, she was promoted to Computer Security Division Chief for NIST. She holds a master's degree in computer science from Virginia Tech. Welcome.

Our second witness is Mr. David Shive, Chief Information Officer at the U.S. General Services Administration. Prior to being named CIO, Mr. Shive was the Director of the Office of Enterprise Infrastructure at the GSA. He received his bachelor's degree in physics from California State University in Fresno, his master's degree in research meteorology from the University of Maryland in College Park, and his postgraduate management certificate from the Carnegie Mellon Graduate School of Industrial Management.

Our third witness is Mr. James Norton. He is the founder and President of Play-Action Strategies LLC, and an Adjunct Professor at Johns Hopkins University. Mr. Norton previously served as Vice President of Strategy and Communications for the Mission Systems Division at General Dynamics. He holds a Bachelor of Science and a master's in business administration from Salve Regina University.

Our last witness today is Mr. Sean Kanuck, Director of Future Conflict and Cyber Security at the International Institute for Strategic Studies. He previously served as the National Intelligence Officer for Cyber Issues from 2011 to 2016. Mr. Kanuck holds a Bachelor of Arts and law degree from Harvard University, a master's of science from the London School of Economics, and an LLM from the University of Oslo.

Thank you all for being here. I will now recognize Ms. Dodson for five minutes to present her testimony.

TESTIMONY OF DONNA DODSON

Ms. Dodson. Chairman LaHood, Ranking Member Beyer, and members of the Subcommittee, I am Donna Dodson, Chief Cybersecurity Advisor for the National Institute of Standards and Technology, known as NIST. Thank you for the opportunity to appear before you today to discuss NIST's role in cybersecurity highlighting the Cybersecurity Framework, referred to as the Framework, and the NIST cybersecurity portfolio.

As a non-regulatory agency, NIST leverages its deep technical expertise as well as its power of convener of stakeholders to develop and improve solutions to a wide range of technical and policy cybersecurity challenges. NIST's role in cybersecurity as codified in law is to research, develop, and deploy information security standards and technology to protect the federal government's non-national security information systems against threats to confidentiality, integrity, and availability, and to facilitate and support the development of voluntary industry-led cybersecurity standards and best practices for critical infrastructure.

In addition to providing resources that organizations of all sizes can use to manage cybersecurity risk, NIST also provides resources to help organizations recover quickly from cybersecurity attacks with confidence that the recovered data is accurate, complete, and free of malware and that the recovered system is trustworthy and capable.

I will highlight five of NIST's critical cybersecurity programs which are the Cybersecurity Framework, supply-chain risk management, cryptography, the National Vulnerability Database, and the National Software Reference Library.

The first resource, the NIST Cybersecurity Framework, or Framework, was created in collaboration with industry, academia and other government agencies. The Framework consists of voluntary standards, guidelines and practices to promote the protection of critical infrastructure and to manage cybersecurity risks. While originally designed to help protect critical infrastructure, numerous businesses use the Framework to manage their cybersecurity risk. Since publishing the Framework, NIST has released additional guidelines to help small businesses manage their cybersecurity risk. Under Executive Order 13800, every federal agency or department will need to manage their cybersecurity risk by using the Framework and then provide a risk management report to OMB and DHS. In response to the EO, NIST released the Cybersecurity Framework Implementation Guidance for Federal Agencies to help federal agencies use the Framework in conjunction with an extensive set of NIST cybersecurity risk management standards, guidelines, and controls to manage their cybersecurity risk.

The Cybersecurity Framework also provides guidance for the second critical area, which is the security of the supply chain. Because of outsourcing, organizations must ensure the integrity, security, and resilience of their supply chain. To assist in this, NIST established the Supply Chain Risk Management program to identify and evaluate effective technologies, tools, techniques, practices, and standards that help secure an organization's supply chain.

Another critical area is cryptography. NIST began its work in cryptography in 1972. Today, NIST cryptographers research, analyze and standardize cryptographic technology. Although these standards apply to federal information systems, many private-sector organizations voluntarily rely on them to protect sensitive personal and business information. NIST also runs a program that validates the test results of vendor's cryptographic modules to the NIST standard. In this program, NIST confirms that a company's underlying cryptography works but is not validating the vendor or the company.

Two final critical components are the National Vulnerability Database and the National Software Reference Library. NIST maintains the repository for all known and publicly reported IT vulnerabilities called the National Vulnerability Database, or NVD. The vulnerabilities in the NVD are weaknesses in coding found in software and hardware that if exploited can impact the integrity of information systems. The National Software Reference Library, or NSRL, is another tool that along with DHS and other, federal, state and local enforcement agencies is supported by the NIST. The NSRL is like a fingerprint database for computer files that promotes efficient and effective use of computer technology.

The programs that I have mentioned here are only a portion of NIST portfolio and cybersecurity NIST worked to provide and improve technical and policy solutions to an ever-growing set of cyber-security challenges continues to grow.

Thank you for the opportunity to testify today. I am happy to answer any questions you may have.

[The prepared statement of Ms. Dodson follows:]

21

Testimony of

Donna Dodson
Chief Cybersecurity Advisor
Director, National Cybersecurity Center of Excellence
National Institute of Standards and Technology
United States Department of Commerce

Before the
United States House of Representatives
Committee on Science, Space, and Technology
Subcommittee on Oversight

"Bolstering the Government's Cybersecurity: Assessing the Risk of Kaspersky Lab Products to the Federal Government"

October 25, 2017

Introduction

Chairman LaHood, Ranking Member Beyer, and members of the Subcommittee, I am Donna Dodson, Director of the National Cybersecurity Center of Excellence and Chief Cybersecurity Advisor at the Department of Commerce's National Institute of Standards and Technology (NIST). Thank you for the opportunity to appear before you today to discuss NIST's key roles in cybersecurity. Specifically, I will discuss NIST's activities in support of the cybersecurity Framework and NIST's cybersecurity portfolio.

NIST's Role in Cybersecurity

NIST is a non-regulatory agency with the mission to promote U.S. innovation and industrial competitiveness in ways that enhance economic security and improve our quality of life. As a non-regulatory agency, NIST leverages its deep technical expertise, as well as its power as a convener of stakeholders from government, academia, and the private sector to develop and improve solutions to a wide range of technical and policy cybersecurity challenges.

One of NIST's key roles is to research, develop, and deploy information security standards and technology to protect the Federal Government's information systems against threats to confidentiality, integrity, and availability. Such efforts were strengthened through the Computer Security Act of 1987 (*Public Law 100-235*), broadened through the Federal Information Security Management Act of 2002 (FISMA*) (Public Law 107-347*), and reaffirmed in the Federal Information Security Modernization Act of 2014 (*Public Law 113-283*). The Cybersecurity Enhancement Act of 2014 (*Public Law 113-274*) further authorized NIST to facilitate and support the development of voluntary, industry-led cybersecurity standards and best practices for critical infrastructure.

To address cybersecurity issues, NIST has long worked effectively with industry and federal agencies to help protect the confidentiality, integrity, and availability of information systems. NIST's Information Technology Laboratory (ITL) develops and deploys standards, tests, and metrics to make the nation's information systems more secure, usable, interoperable, and reliable. Our work in the cybersecurity area covers program areas including configuration and vulnerability management, cryptography, cybersecurity education and workforce development, identity and access management and risk management.

In addition to providing resources that organizations of all sizes can use to manage cybersecurity risk, NIST also provides resources to help organizations recover quickly from cybersecurity attacks with confidence that the recovered data is accurate, complete, and free of malware and that the recovered system trustworthy and fully capable to again function as originally designed. Some of NIST's critical cybersecurity resources are described below.

NIST's Cybersecurity Framework

In 2014, NIST issued the *Framework for Improving Critical Infrastructure Cybersecurity*[1] (Framework), which NIST created in collaboration with industry, academia, and other

---

[1] https://www.nist.gov/cyberframework

government agencies. The Framework consists of voluntary standards, guidelines, and practices to promote the protection of critical infrastructure, such as the information technology, transportation, energy, healthcare, and financial services sectors. The voluntary, risk-based, flexible, repeatable, and cost-effective approach of the Framework helps those who use the Framework to manage cybersecurity risk. The Framework was originally designed to help protect critical infrastructure, but numerous business of all sizes and from many economic sectors now use the Framework to manage their cybersecurity risks, such as for supply chain risk management as described below.

Since publishing the Framework, NIST has released the NIST Interagency Report (NISTIR) *Small Business Information Security: The Fundamentals* (NISTIR 7621) to help small businesses understand and manage their cybersecurity risks.

Under Executive Order 13800, *Strengthening the Cybersecurity of Federal Networks and Critical Infrastructure*, signed by President Trump on May 11, 2017, every Federal agency or department has to manage their cybersecurity risk by using the Framework and provide a risk management report to the Director of the Office of Management and Budget and to the Secretary of Homeland Security.

NIST also released a draft NISTIR, *The Cybersecurity Framework: Implementation Guidance for Federal Agencies* (NISTIR 8170). This report helps federal agencies use the Framework, in conjunction with an extensive set of NIST cybersecurity risk management standards, guidelines, and controls, to manage their cybersecurity risks. Currently, NIST is in the process of updating the Framework, a process NIST plans to finalize in 2018.

NIST collaborates with the Department of Homeland Security's (DHS) Critical Infrastructure Cyber Community Voluntary Program to promote Framework implementation within the critical infrastructure sectors. NIST and DHS coordinate on a range of events promoting Framework implementation and understanding, such as webinars and workshops.

Supply Chain Risk Management

The Cybersecurity Framework also provides guidance for the security of the supply chain and to reduce supply chain threats to businesses and the manufacturing sector. The number of information and communication technologies is rapidly increasing and becoming more capable and complex every day. These technologies rely on a supply-chain ecosystem that is long, complex, variable, interconnected, globally distributed, and geographically diverse. Many organizations outsource the development, maintenance, and management of this ecosystem.

Because of this outsourcing, organizations—including federal agencies—are increasingly at risk of supply chain compromise. The same factors that decrease cost, enable interoperability, foster rapid innovation, and provide other benefits, also increase cyber supply chain risks. Managing supply chain risk requires an organization to ensure the integrity, security, and resilience of its supply chain.

NIST developed the Supply Chain Risk Management Program to work with industry, academia, and government to identify and evaluate effective technologies, tools, techniques, practices, and standards that help secure an organization's supply chain. This program examines the supply-chain risk throughout the entire lifecycle of systems, products, and services.

NIST is currently working to describe a structured method of prioritizing systems and components based on their relationship to an organization's mission, thereby enabling organizations to most efficiently deploy their resources.

Cryptography

NIST began its work on cryptography in 1972 and its importance is reflected in the growth of this work today. Under FISMA, NIST is responsible for developing standards and guidelines to protect non-national security federal information systems and the information they process. Our Cryptographic Technology Group (CTG) researches, analyzes, and standardizes cryptographic techniques and technologies, while encouraging innovation and helping technology users manage risks.

Although Federal Information Processing Standards (FIPS) apply to federal information systems, many private sector organizations voluntarily rely on them to protect sensitive personal and business information.

The Cryptographic Technology Group is developing its standards using an open and transparent process. The CTG conducts workshops and requests input and comments from government agencies, private industry, academia, and the global cryptographic community. We make such comments available publicly in the interest of transparency, trust, and to promote future research. The CTG examines each of its standards on a regular basis to determine if they need to be revised, withdrawn, or re-opened for public comment and, when appropriate, possible revision.

In addition to developing these standards, NIST runs the Cryptographic Module Validation Program, which validates the test results of a vendor's cryptographic modules to NIST FIPS 140-2. Laboratories accredited under the program test any company's cryptography to determine whether it meets NIST's cryptographic standards. NIST does not "pick winners and losers" among potential vendors. Rather, private-sector accredited testing laboratories conduct testing under this program that simply confirms whether a company's underlying cryptography works and technically meets the standard—nothing more and nothing less. As with the FIPS standards themselves, many private sector organizations worldwide rely upon this testing program for assurance that the cryptographic products they purchase meet NIST standards. To date, under this voluntary testing program, over 3000 cryptographic modules have been successfully validated under this program.

The National Vulnerability Database

Protecting information technology is critical and NIST plays a key role in this area by maintaining the repository of all known and publicly reported information technology vulnerabilities, called the National Vulnerability Database (NVD). The NVD is an authoritative source for standardized information on security vulnerabilities that NIST updates regularly.

These vulnerabilities catalogued in the NVD are weaknesses in coding found in software and hardware that, if exploited, can impact the confidentiality, integrity, or availability of information or information systems. The NVD tracks vulnerabilities over time and allows users to assess changes in vulnerability discovery rates within specific products or specific types of vulnerabilities.

As part of maintaining the NVD, NIST works with organizations that apply to become a Common Vulnerabilities and Exposures (CVE) Numbering Authority, which allows an organization to publicly disclose a vulnerability with a preassigned CVE ID number, rather than be required to request a new number every time it discovers a new vulnerability. NIST also analyzes and provides a severity metric to assist practitioners in responding to each vulnerability.

National Software Reference Library

NIST, along with the Department of Homeland Security, and other federal, state, and local law enforcement agencies, supports the National Software Reference Library (NSRL). The NSRL collects digital signatures of software so that an organization can efficiently search its networks for that software and determine if and where the software is deployed. In a sense, the NSRL is like a fingerprint database for computer files; however, rather than helping a detective identify a person, it helps an organization quickly find a piece of software. In effect, the NSRL promotes efficient and effective use of computer technology in the investigation of crimes involving computers.

The NSRL collects software from various sources and incorporates profiles computed from this software into a Reference Data Set (RDS) of information. The RDS can be used by law enforcement, government, and private industry to review files on a computer by matching profiles in the RDS. This process helps alleviate much of the effort involved in determining which files on a computer are important evidence or which files are already part of a criminal investigation. This ability reduces the number of files which must be manually examined, reducing the time and other resources law enforcement officials need to commit to a single incident.

Other stakeholders, such as businesses and other government agencies, use the NSRL RDS as part of their routine IT operations to ensure there are no malicious or unverified files on their systems.

Conclusion

The programs that I have mentioned here are only a portion of NIST's portfolio in cybersecurity, which is only a portion of what NIST does more broadly. NIST's work to provide and improve technical and policy solutions to an ever-growing set of cybersecurity challenges continues to grow. Thank you for the opportunity to testify today on NIST's work in cybersecurity. I am happy to answer any questions you may have.

Donna F. Dodson, NIST Associate Director and Chief Cyber Security Advisor

Donna F. Dodson is a Fellow at the National Institute of Standards and Technology (NIST). She holds the position of the Chief Cybersecurity Advisor for NIST and is the Associate Director for the Information Technology Lab (ITL). Donna also serves as the Director of NIST's National Cybersecurity Center of Excellence (NCCoE).

Donna oversees ITL's cyber security program to conduct research, development and outreach necessary to provide standards, guidelines, tools, metrics and practices to protect the information and communication infrastructure. Under her leadership, ITL collaborations with industry, academia and other government agencies in research areas such as security management and assurance, cryptography and systems security, identity management, security automation, secure system and component configuration, test validation and measurement of security properties of products and systems, security awareness and outreach and emerging security technologies. In addition, Donna guides ITL programs to support both national and international security standards activities. She recently led the establishment of the NIST NCCoE. Through partnerships with state, local and industry, the NCCoE collaborates with industry sectors to accelerate the widespread adoption of standards-based cyber security tools and technologies.

Donna's research interests include applied cryptography, key management, authentication and security testing. She has led technical teams to produce standards, guidelines and tools in each of these areas.

Donna received two Department of Commerce Gold Medals and three NIST Bronze Medals. She was a Fed 100 Award winner for her innovations in cybersecurity and in 2011 was included in the top 10 influential people in government information security. Recently, FedScoop recognized Donna as one of DC's Top 50 Women in Tech.

Chairman LaHood. Thank you, Ms. Dodson.

I now recognize Mr. Shive for five minutes to present his testimony.

TESTIMONY OF DAVID SHIVE

Mr. Shive. Thank you, and good morning, Chairman LaHood, Ranking Member Beyer, and members of the Subcommittee. My name is David Shive, and I'm the Chief Information Officer at the U.S. General Services Administration. I welcome the opportunity to share my organization's experiences related to the cybersecurity posture of GSA and the federal government.

The mission of GSA is to deliver the best value in real estate, acquisition, and technology services to government and the American people. In support of that, one of my organization's key goals in supporting GSA's mission is to deliver technology that provides both a secure environment for doing business while also ensuring that both IT and business continue to run efficiently.

The Federal Information Security Management Act provides a comprehensive framework which helps federal CIOs and federal Chief Information Security Officers manage overall information technology security risks across federal data and assets. The FISMA framework supports the rigorous IT security program implemented at GSA by the CISO under the auspices of the CIO's authority. Our security program assures the risks to GSA's IT systems are assessed and proper security controls implemented to mitigate those risks down to an acceptable level. It also ensures periodic evaluation and testing of the effectiveness of IT security controls, including management, operational, and technical controls.

Furthermore, GSA has a robust incident handling and response program that strongly aligns with the NIST Cybersecurity Framework. Due to the effectiveness of that program, GSA received a rating level of 4, which is managed and measurable under "response" on the latest FISMA report from our Office of the Inspector General (OIG).

In accordance with FISMA, GSA adheres to all of NIST's Federal Information Processing Standards and Special Publications in implementing GSA's IT security program. In addition, GSA completes a risk-based security assessment in accordance with NIST guidance and issues a signed Authority to Operate by the authorizing official with concurrence by the CISO before any new system goes into production. This is accomplished by prioritizing the implementation of security controls and focusing on those that have the biggest impact on securing the system and data such as securing—ensuring secure configurations and patching of vulnerabilities, access controls, and auditing and monitoring. GSA is in the process of implementing Executive Order 13800. GSA has adopted the framework for Improving Critical Infrastructure Cybersecurity developed by NIST and has required—as required by the Executive Order. GSA has provided a risk management report, as well as an action plan to implement the Framework, to the Secretary of Homeland Security and the Director of the Office of Management and Budget. GSA continues to explore leading edge technologies in order to stop the latest and most sophisticated attacks from our adversaries.

This includes next generation antivirus solutions that use machine learning and artificial intelligence, as well as advanced detection of malware that is embedded in email attachments and links. Both of these technologies will greatly protect the end user, which is one of the primary vectors for exploiting federal government systems.

One of GSA's core missions is to assist in procuring goods and services that can be made available to federal agencies. GSA's Federal Acquisition Service (FAS) offers a continuum of voluntary government-wide innovative solutions and services in a number of areas. Federal agencies spend approximately $23 billion annually to acquire IT products and services through FAS. This represents only 42 percent of the federal government's $55 billion in total IT spend. Significantly, a product's placement on a GSA schedule or contract vehicle only certifies that the vendor meets the necessary regulatory requirements for the product to be sold to the federal government. It does not make any value or technical judgment about the nature of the product.

With respect to Kaspersky Lab products, they were available from three resale vendors on GSA schedules contracts. On July 11 of this year, GSA directed the three resellers to remove all Kaspersky Lab manufactured products from their catalogs within 30 days. All three resellers complied. As of today, GSA does not offer any Kaspersky Lab manufactured products through its our GSA scheduled contracts.

GSA took a proactive stance and completed comprehensive scanning of all IT assets for the presence of Kaspersky products in June of 2017. GSA confirmed that there was no installation of such products in our on-premise and cloud-based systems, and reported this to DHS in accordance with Binding Operational Directive) 17–01 on October 4. In addition, GSA's FedRAMP PMO is coordinating this activity for the government-wide cloud service providers that are covered by its ATOs.

Again, I thank the Subcommittee for its oversight and for allowing me the opportunity to contribute to this important topic. At this time, I'm happy to take any questions that you might have.

[The prepared statement of Mr. Shive follows:]

10/25/2017 Hearing: Cybersecurity Posture
The Oversight Subcommittee of the
Committee on Science, Space, and Technology of the
U.S. House of Representatives

Introduction

Good morning Chairman LaHood, Ranking Member Beyer, and members of the Subcommittee. My name is David Shive, and I am the Chief Information Officer (CIO) of the U.S. General Services Administration (GSA). I welcome the opportunity to share my organization's experiences related to the cybersecurity posture of the Federal Government, specifically pertaining to the utilization of Kaspersky Lab products at Federal agencies, as well as the implementation of Executive Order 13800 and the NIST Cybersecurity Framework.

GSA Mission

The mission of GSA is to deliver the best value in real estate, acquisition, and technology services to Government and the American people. GSA's priorities are to deliver better value and savings, serve our partners, expand opportunities for small business, make Government more sustainable, and be a leader in innovation.

In support of that, and as it relates to the Subcommittee's objectives today, one of my organization's key goals in supporting GSA's mission is to deliver technology that provides a secure environment for doing business, while ensuring that both IT and business continue to run efficiently.

FISMA

The Federal Information Security Modernization Act of 2014 (FISMA) provides a comprehensive framework which helps Federal CIOs and Federal Chief Information Security Officers (CISOs) manage overall Information Technology (IT) security risks across Federal data and assets.

The FISMA framework supports the rigorous IT security program implemented at GSA by the CISO under the auspices of the CIO's authority. Our security program assures risks to GSA's IT systems are assessed and proper security controls implemented to mitigate those risks down to an acceptable level. It also provides a comprehensive policy, procedure, and governance structure, and ensures periodic evaluation and testing of the effectiveness of IT security controls, including management, operational, and technical controls. Further, all GSA employees take IT security awareness training; role-based training may also be required dependent on position and function.

Furthermore, GSA has a robust incident handling and response program that strongly aligns with the NIST Cybersecurity Framework. Due to the effectiveness of that program, GSA received a rating of Level 4 (Managed and Measurable) under "Response" on the latest FISMA report from the Office of Inspector General (OIG).

NIST Standards, FISMA and ATOs

In accordance with FISMA, GSA adheres to all of NIST's Federal Information Processing Standards (FIPS) and Special Publications (SP) in implementing GSA's IT security program. These include standards and guidance on encryption, security categorization of confidentiality, integrity, and availability (i.e., low, moderate, high), security control selection and implementation, risk management, authentication, identity management, system authorization, and contingency planning.

In addition, GSA completes a risk-based security assessment in accordance with NIST guidance and issues a signed Authority to Operate (ATO) by the authorizing official with concurrence by the CISO before any new system goes into production. The ATO is the official declaration that the IT systems can go live and be operated within an acceptable level of risk.

Cybersecurity Risk Management

Using the FISMA framework, along with NIST's Cybersecurity Framework, standards, and publications, GSA implements a risk-based strategy to manage IT security across the enterprise. Risk can never be completely eliminated, but the goal of GSA's IT security program is to allow GSA to provide services to its customers using information technology operated within an acceptable level of risk. This is accomplished by prioritizing the implementation of the security controls and focusing on those that have the biggest impact on securing the system and data. These include, but are not limited to: encryption, 2-factor authentication, ensuring secure configurations and patching of vulnerabilities, access controls, and auditing and monitoring.

Implementation of EO 13800 and the NIST Cybersecurity Framework

GSA is in the process of implementing Executive Order 13800, *Strengthening the Cybersecurity of Federal Networks and Critical Infrastructure* (May 11, 2017). GSA has adopted the framework for Improving Critical Infrastructure Cybersecurity (the Framework) developed by the National Institute of Standards and Technology, as required by the Executive Order. Specifically, GSA uses the Identify, Protect, Detect, Respond, and Recover areas of the NIST cybersecurity framework to better manage the overall risk to the agency.

In addition, GSA has provided a risk management report, as well as an action plan to implement the Framework, to the Secretary of Homeland Security and the Director of the Office of Management and Budget (OMB) per the Executive Order. The report identified GSA's highest risk areas along with risk mitigation and acceptance choices. GSA's program received an overall evaluation of "Managing Risk" by the U.S. Department of Homeland Security (DHS) in their Cybersecurity Risk Management Assessment as part of the Executive Order.

GSA continues to explore leading edge technologies in order to stop the latest and most sophisticated attacks from our adversaries. These include next generation anti-virus solutions that use machine learning and artificial intelligence, as well as advanced detection of malware that is embedded in email attachments and links. This is done by doing in-depth analysis of the email before it reaches the end user. Both of these technologies will greatly protect the end user which is one of the primary vectors for exploiting Federal Government systems (otherwise known as phishing attacks).

GSA Role in Governmentwide IT Procurement

One of GSA's core missions is to assist in procuring goods and services that can be made available to Federal agencies. GSA's Federal Acquisition Service (FAS) offers a continuum of Governmentwide innovative solutions and services in a number of areas. Federal agencies spend approximately $23 billion annually to acquire IT products and services through FAS. This amount represents only 42 percent of the $54.8 billion in total contracted Federal IT spending across the entire Federal Government. As this figure indicates, Federal agencies are not required to use GSA contracts and, in fact, the majority of Federal IT spending does not occur through GSA.

Regardless of the acquisition vehicle used to acquire IT, as CIO it is my responsibility, as is the responsibility of any agency CIO, to ensure that we conduct a thorough examination of the IT solution and understand the risk of the product before we interface it with the existing agency IT infrastructure.

Significantly, a product's placement on a GSA Multiple Award Schedule (Schedule) or other contract vehicle only certifies that the vendor meets the necessary contract and legal authority requirements for the product to be sold to the Federal Government; it does not make any value or technical judgment about the nature of the product. In the IT space, FISMA requires agency CIOs, such as myself, to make the determination for which products and solutions are appropriate for an agency's environment.

With respect to Kaspersky Lab (KL) products, three resellers offered KL products through GSA Schedules contracts, but did not gain approval to do so via the required contract modification process. On July 11, 2017, GSA directed the three resellers to remove all KL manufactured products from their catalogs within 30 days. All three resellers complied. In addition, it is GSA's understanding that on the same day, NASA and NIH, the other two Federal agencies with Governmentwide IT procurement contracts, removed Kaspersky manufactured products from their resellers' catalogs. GSA does not offer any Kaspersky Lab manufactured products through its Schedules contracts.

Discovery and Removal of Kaspersky Products

GSA took a proactive stance and completed comprehensive scanning of all IT assets for the presence of KL products in June 2017. GSA confirmed that there was no installation of KL products in GSA's on-premise and cloud-based systems, and reported this to DHS in accordance with its Binding Operational Directive (BOD) 17-01 on October 4, 2017. GSA currently uses McAfee as its anti-virus provider.

In addition, GSA's Federal Risk and Authorization Management Program's (FedRAMP) Program Management Office is coordinating this activity for the Governmentwide Cloud Service Providers (CSPs) that are covered by FedRAMP ATOs.

Conclusion

Again, I thank you for allowing me the opportunity to contribute to this important topic. GSA appreciates this Committee's oversight of the Federal Government's cybersecurity posture on behalf of the American people.

At this time, I'm happy to take any questions that you might have.

David A. Shive, *Chief Information Officer for the U.S. General Services Administration*

David A. Shive is the Chief Information Officer for the U.S. General Services Administration. Mr. Shive oversees the GSA IT organization, and is responsible information technology operations and ensuring alignment with agency and administration strategic objectives and priorities. He joined the U.S. General Services Administration's Office of the Chief Information Officer in November 2012. Prior to being named CIO, he was the Associate CIO of the Office of Enterprise Infrastructure, responsible for the enterprise information technology infrastructure platforms and capability that support the GSA business enterprise. He was also the ACIO for Corporate Systems for the GSA business support offices. Prior to joining GSA, he served in the District of Columbia government as a Chief Information Officer. In this role, Mr. Shive had executive responsibility for agency IT operations including financial systems, security and privacy programs, internal controls and compliance, strategic planning, enterprise architecture and performance management and measurement programs and directed the transformation of enterprise systems and processes. to public/private cloud hybrid. He holds an undergraduate degree in physics from California State University. Fresno; a master's degree in research meteorology from the University of Maryland College Park; and a post-graduate management certificate from the Carnegie Mellon Graduate School of Industrial Management.

Chairman LaHood. Thank you, Mr. Shive.

At this time I recognize Mr. Norton for five minutes to present his testimony.

TESTIMONY OF JAMES NORTON

Mr. Norton. Thank you. Chairman LaHood, Ranking Member Beyer, and members of the Subcommittee, thank you very much for inviting me to testify before you today. My name is James Norton, and I am the founder and President of Play-Action Strategies, a homeland security and cybersecurity consulting firm here in Washington, DC. I'm also a member of the faculty at Johns Hopkins University.

Previously, I served in multiple positions at the Department of Homeland Security under President George W. Bush including as Deputy Assistant Secretary of Legislation Affairs. I was a member of the Department's first team tasked with confronting the nascent cybersecurity threat.

Cyber threats pose a real and immediate danger to our federal government and the American people it represents. In 2016, the federal government experienced 30,899 cyber incidents that led to the compromise of information or system functionality according to the Office of Management and Budget.

DHS's role in protecting government networks is foundational. Because the Department cannot be well positioned to assist the private sector and serve as a model of best practices for state and local governments until it has its own federal networks or federal systems secure. In order to meet today's challenges, DHS must update its systems and technology and strengthen the organization in support of its cybersecurity functions. Together these issues have led to the use of potentially problematic software that is the subject of today's hearing.

To help DHS meaningfully address these challenges, I offer the following recommendations: provide CIOs and other officials across federal agencies with the resources necessary to invest in high-quality, reliable cybersecurity tools; require the development of a trusted vendor list that provides guidance on approved cybersecurity vendors with a secure supply chain that agencies can have confidence in; work with OMB and the White House to prevent redundancy across the federal government so that competing cyber organizations do not arise in other federal agencies.

I thank the Committee for holding this important hearing, and I look forward to your questions.

[The prepared statement of Mr. Norton follows:]

Subcommittee on Oversight Hearing - Bolstering the Government's Cybersecurity: Assessing the Risk of Kaspersky Lab Products to the Federal Government

U.S. House of Representatives Committee on Science, Space, and Technology
Subcommittee on Oversight

Testimony of James Norton
Founder and President, Play-Action Strategies LLC

October 25, 2017

Introduction

Chairman LaHood, Ranking Member Beyer, and members of the Subcommittee, thank you very much for inviting me to testify before you today.

My name is James Norton, and I am the founder and president of Play-Action Strategies LLC, a homeland security and cybersecurity consulting firm here in Washington, D.C. Previously, I served in multiple positions at the Department of Homeland Security ("DHS") under President George W. Bush, including as Deputy Assistant Secretary of Legislative Affairs. During the stand up of DHS, I was involved in policy formation and execution related to border security, aviation, and infrastructure protection. I was also deeply engaged in the creation of the Department's first team dedicated to confronting the then-nascent cybersecurity threat. After my service at DHS, I continued to work extensively on cybersecurity issues in my consultancy and as an adjunct faculty member at Johns Hopkins University's Zanvyl Krieger School of Arts and Sciences Advanced Academic Programs, teaching courses on homeland security, cybersecurity policy, and congressional affairs.[1] To be clear however, today I am expressing my personal

---

[1] The views expressed today are solely my own and are not representative of Johns Hopkins or any other organization.

views. I am appearing in my individual capacity and not as a representative of any company or organization.

The Department's mission is stated simply—"With honor and integrity, we will safeguard the American people, our homeland, and our values"—but in practice it is anything but. To be successful, DHS must be dynamic and possess the ability to evolve ahead of the ever-changing threats we face. It is important to note that DHS was created in response to the devastating terror attacks of September 11, 2001, and, as such, it initially focused on physical threats to the homeland. Emergency management was also a core function of the Department from its inception. But securing the homeland took on additional meaning as cyber attacks emerged as one of the most serious threats to our national security. Over time, the Department has taken on the dual functions of protecting federal civilian networks and of building cybersecurity partnerships with private sector stakeholders. The Department has done an admirable job, and its recent efforts, working with the private sector to blunt the impact of the WannaCry ransomware attack is just one example of its fine work in the cyber arena.

As the Committee is well aware, however, more work remains. The focus of my testimony will be on the internal side of DHS's cyber mission, which is to protect government networks. This portion of DHS's mission is foundational, because the Department cannot be well-positioned to assist the private sector and serve as a model of best practices for state and local governments until it has its own federal systems secure. Additional resources and legislative fixes will be critical in equipping the Department to carry out its mission.

Current Cyber Threat Landscape

Cyber threats pose a real and immediate danger to our federal government and the American people it represents. The increasing volume and sophistication of cyber attacks puts the sensitive information, taxpayer money, and critical systems controlled by the federal government at serious risk. We have seen dramatic and far-reaching consequences from cyber attacks on the federal government in recent years. In 2015, a data breach at the federal Office of Personnel Management exposed the personal information of more than 20 million current, former, and prospective federal employees and contractors.[2] But, only a tiny fraction of cybersecurity incidents garner media attention. The unfortunate reality is that breaches within and attacks on federal government systems are pervasive. In 2016, the federal government experienced 30,899 cyber incidents that led to the compromise of information or system functionality, according to a report from the Office of Management and Budget.[3] Moreover, federal agencies faced thousands of other attempted intrusions that were ultimately unsuccessful.

Importance of Hearing

This hearing comes at a critical moment. Those of us who follow cybersecurity issues have long wondered when the tipping point will be reached. That is, when does the cyber threat become real and tangible enough for us to stop being reactionary and finally dedicate sufficient resources and talent to get ahead of it? I believe that moment is now, and I thank the Committee for its important and continuing work in providing coherence and funding to federal cybersecurity efforts. The Department is resilient and, with the help of Congress, it has dramatically improved its capacities in other areas: Aviation security and emergency

---

[2] "OPM Hack: Government Finally Starts Notifying 21.5 Million Victims," NBC News, 10/1/2015
[3] Federal Information Security Modernization Act of 2014 Annual Report to Congress – FY2016, Office of Management and Budget, November 2016

management, for example. The same can happen with cybersecurity. With guidance, support, and funding from Congress, DHS could provide the federal civilian network protection that the American people need and deserve.

Challenges at the Federal Level

The first hurdle DHS must clear is the update of its systems and technology. The scope of the cybersecurity challenge has grown exponentially over the past decade. The Government Accountability Office (GAO) found that the number of annual information security incidents affecting the federal government has grown by more than 1,300 percent since fiscal year 2006.[4] But the cybersecurity infrastructure at the federal level has not kept pace. While I served at DHS, one of my responsibilities was to work as a DHS representative with the initial group of individuals at the national cyber security division to establish relationships with the other agencies, the private sector, and leaders on Capitol Hill to create the early cybersecurity framework to guide departmental operations. Programs that are still in operation today – like Einstein, which detects and blocks cyber attacks and allows DHS to use threat information detected in one agency to protect the rest of the government – were born during those early days and, unfortunately, the Department is still using technology and strategy from 15 years ago. The GAO recently concluded, "Einstein was largely ineffective at thwarting hackers" because it "could only detect known cyber threats and lacked the ability to suss out sophisticated hackers."[5]

Another challenge to be addressed is the organization of DHS's cybersecurity function. The cyber organization was initially buried in the now-defunct Information

---

[4] Testimony Before the Subcommittee on Research and Technology, Committee on Science, Space, and Technology, House of Representatives – Cybersecurity: Actions Needed to Strengthen US Capabilities, United States Government Accountability Office, 2/14/2017
[5] "DHS cyber chief defends expansion of criticized software," The Hill, 2/11/2016

Analysis and Infrastructure Protection bureaucracy. When DHS was reorganized in the wake of Hurricane Katrina, several agencies, including the Office of Biometric Identity Management, the Federal Protective Service and the cyber functions, were left without a home and were all grouped together into a new sub-organization at DHS called the National Protection and Programs Directorate (NPPD). As a result, it is not apparent from the cybersecurity operation's organizational status that cybersecurity is a top priority for DHS. Cybersecurity operations lack the organizational muscle, credibility and political support they need in order to lead on cyber. For example, the procurement of the more than one billion dollar "Domino" program was delayed for almost three years, undermining DHS' ability to increase its cybersecurity capacity. DHS should be reorganized to create a standalone cybersecurity component agency; a critical first step is the appointment of an Undersecretary of NPPD who can serve as a point person for the Department's cyber functions.

This important hearing is focused on the removal of potentially problematic software – this issue is partly the result of massive confusion about who, specifically, is in charge at DHS. Without a dedicated cyber organization to set policy, different Chief Information Officers (CIOs) are independently responsible for purchasing software and other cybersecurity tools – leading to a system that relies on many different products with differing levels of quality and security. Reorganization would allow cybersecurity authority to be both concentrated within the Department—in the leadership of a standalone agency—and exerted across DHS and the federal civilian operations—through cybersecurity leadership that possesses the requisite authority and clout.

Returning to software acquisitions, a compounding factor to the current challenge is the fact that – as a result of sequestration – many CIOs are forced to abide by the lowest price technically acceptable (LPTA) standard, which often means they don't end up with the best products. In order to have a first-class civilian cyber organization, the Federal government needs to spend money and provide consistent guidance on high-quality, secure products. Funding is a key issue when it comes to cybersecurity infrastructure across the federal government. When President Trump signed an Executive Order ("EO") 13800 - "Strengthening the Cybersecurity of Federal Networks and Critical Infrastructure" – he indicated a commendable focus on the security of federal networks. Two key provisions of the EO are the requirement that all Federal agencies use the National Institute of Standards and Technology Cybersecurity Framework and the direction to all federal agencies to identify ways to improve cybersecurity in critical infrastructure. But without funding, these well-intended orders become unenforceable mandates. The protection of federal civilian networks therefore hinges on support and funding that must be initiated in this Chamber.

Recommendations

In the face of rapidly increasing and evolving threats to cyber infrastructure, there are certain concrete steps Congress and the federal government can take to protect critical systems:

1. There is currently legislation pending – H.R.3359, the Cybersecurity and Infrastructure Security Agency Act of 2017 – that would reorganize DHS and create a dedicated cyber agency. Centralizing civilian cyber operations within

DHS will create a more coherent chain of command for addressing cybersecurity issues and will help leverage limited resources more effectively. Establishing a trusted organization that has research and development capabilities, and the ability to share information in real time will only be possible with a new, fully-funded organization. Congress should act quickly to implement such a reorganization.

2. Budget cuts across the Federal government – specifically as a result of sequestration – have forced CIOs and other officials to rely on the lowest price technically acceptable (LPTA) standard when acquiring cybersecurity software and other tools. When it comes to critical cybersecurity infrastructure, sacrificing quality for short-term savings has the potential to leave open vulnerabilities and cost more money in the long-term as a result of intrusions. CIOs and other officials across federal agencies should be empowered with the resources necessary to invest in high-quality, reliable cybersecurity tools.

3. The quality of cybersecurity software and other tools is tremendously important, but there are many different options available to federal, state, and local officials. As the current situation demonstrates, implementing problematic software and later removing it creates significant disruption. The federal government should take the lead on developing a "trusted vendor" list that provides guidance on approved cybersecurity vendors with a secure supply chain that agencies can have confidence in. While this list should

certainly consider the risks associated with sourcing foreign cybersecurity tools, it should recognize that many trusted allies produce high-quality products that would benefit the United States.

4. Prevent Redundancy - The White House, Office of Management and Budget and the Congress should work together to prevent redundancy across the federal government so that competing cyber organizations do not arise in other federal agencies and, instead, centralize federal resources in DHS.

Conclusion

Thank you very much for the opportunity to testify, and I welcome your questions.

James Norton
Founder and President, Play-Action Strategies LLC

James Norton is the Founder and President of Play-Action Strategies LLC, a comprehensive strategic consulting firm located in Washington, D.C.

Previously, James served in multiple positions at the U.S. Department of Homeland Security (DHS), including as Deputy Assistant Secretary of Legislative Affairs, where he was responsible for helping to develop and implement critical policies related to border security, aviation, and infrastructure protection, including the creation of DHS' first cybersecurity team.

James has also previously served as a senior defense-industry executive and as a Special Assistant to U.S. Environmental Protection Agency Administrator Christine Todd Whitman. Since 2008, he has taught graduate level courses on homeland security, cybersecurity policy, and congressional affairs as an Adjunct Professor in the Johns Hopkins University Zanvyl Krieger School of Arts and Sciences.

James has received distinguished awards from both the Environmental Protection Agency and DHS for his government service.

Originally from Massachusetts, James holds Bachelor of Science and Master of Business Administration degrees from Salve Regina University.

James can be reached at James.Norton@playaction.com.

Chairman LaHood. Thank you, Mr. Norton.

At this time I recognize Mr. Kanuck for five minutes to present his testimony.

TESTIMONY OF SEAN KANUCK

Mr. Kanuck. Good morning. Thank you, Chairman LaHood, Ranking Member Beyer, and Distinguished Members of Congress. It's my pleasure to be here today, and being a strategic threat analyst, I'm going to speak directly to the risks theoretically posed by Kaspersky Lab and Russian cyber operations.

First, I think we need to understand the very nature of the technologies that Kaspersky products offer. They are complete network monitoring solutions that can see all activity on their clients' networks, and they have remote administration capabilities. In these ways, they are not dissimilar from many other IT security vendors' products, but what is important to note here is that discussions about surreptitious backdoors in these kind of products is actually a fairly moot point because the very nature of these products and services is to have a wide-open front door. Clients pay for that 24/7 monitoring of their entire network.

Now, what is interesting, that ends up an aggregate providing Kaspersky Lab and other similar vendors incredible optic and visibility into global internet activity including malicious software, espionage activities, and other things. In essence, it becomes a private global cyber intelligence network, and as we've seen from the recent media reports this month, that kind of capability is incredibly desired by government intelligence actors. If we believe the media reports in the public sector, then at least two foreign government agencies have exploited Kaspersky's network, and in my mind, that makes the question of "is there a risk through Kaspersky products" to become nearly tautological because allegedly it's already happened twice.

Furthermore, I do not personally feel it is necessary to prove a willful complicity or collaboration by Kaspersky employees or the company with the Russian government or any other to show that there is a potential risk. That added factor, if it were true, would of course be a counterintelligence concern and a further cause for prohibiting such software or products. But the mere fact alone that foreign intelligence agencies have sought access through this implies there is a risk.

So what I think we need to do is actually focus on that foreign intelligence threat and let's take a moment to discuss Russian cyber posture. I can't do it any justice better than Director of National Intelligence Dan Coats did in his worldwide threat assessment presentation in May where he identified Russia as a primary cyber threat actor of the United States with a continued interest in exploiting our networks not only for espionage but for influence operations, and that testimony further noted that even disruptive actions have been undertaken by Russia against targets outside the United States. So when we combine that willful interest in adversarial context with the telecommunications surveillance and monitoring laws of Russia and the access potentially posed by Kaspersky Lab products, you have a potent combination.

Even without complicity, it is theoretically possible that all Kaspersky Lab corporate communications transiting nodes in Russia could possibly be monitored by the domestic security service under their telecom surveillance laws. Therefore, if you are trying to examine the full scope of this threat, a simple review of Kaspersky's products themselves or the source code would not be enough. You have to understand the commands that remote administrators or unauthorized third parties may be issuing to those client networks through that access point, and you must understand traffic routing of the global internet and how Kaspersky communications move between its regional offices and different counterparts.

Moving to a strategic risk management perspective, I offer that resilience is the key to better security, and my witnesses—my fellow witnesses have already spoken to that to some degree, and I believe that internal review of one's own enterprise assets and who might be trying to compromise them is essential.

I'll conclude by offering a couple thoughts on the prohibition of Kaspersky Lab software in U.S. government networks. I do believe there's a risk posed, and my assessment is primarily based on historical arguments of what has already happened as well as the access that I've described and the foreign threat actors. I am also aware that U.S. government actions against specific named foreign companies may likely result in similar backlashes against U.S. corporate entities. That's not a security risk assessment, it's a political realism.

My last comment will be that I would encourage the U.S. government to assess all IT products from all vendors regardless of national origin because if we're trying to protect sensitive information, we should be fully cognizant that foreign intelligence actors will be willing to exploit any IT vendor that we're using, even if it's not of their own national origin.

Thank you very much.

[The prepared statement of Mr. Kanuck follows:]

STATEMENT FOR THE RECORD

of

Sean Kanuck
Director for Future Conflict and Cyber Security
IISS-Americas

for

United States House of Representatives
Committee on Science, Space, and Technology
Subcommittee on Oversight

Hearing entitled
"Bolstering the Government's Cybersecurity: Assessing the Risk of
Kaspersky Lab Products to the Federal Government"

25 October 2017
10:00 am

Rayburn House Office Building
Room 2318

Chairman LaHood, Ranking Member Beyer, and distinguished Members of Congress:

It is my honor and privilege to participate in the hearing entitled "Bolstering the Government's Cybersecurity: Assessing the Risk of Kaspersky Lab Products to the Federal Government" before the Subcommittee on Oversight of the Committee on Science, Space, and Technology of the House of Representatives. I thank you for your invitation and sincerely hope that my contribution will assist you in your work on this critical topic.

This Statement for the Record draws upon my twenty years of experience in the field of information and communication technologies (ICT), including: as a strategic analyst with the International Institute for Strategic Studies (IISS), as a professional attorney who specializes in cyber law, and formerly, as a senior intelligence officer for the United States Government. Although my testimony today is completely unclassified and provided in my current capacity as a think tank researcher, the perspective offered herein also benefits from my background as the National Intelligence Officer for Cyber Issues from May 2011 to May 2016. Having led cyber threat analysis for the US Intelligence Community for five years, I am quite familiar with assessing the cyber risk to both federal government and critical infrastructure systems.

My testimony will focus on assessing the risk of employing foreign ICT products and services in government networks and attempt to provide a better understanding of how they can be exploited. In my view, the present issue regarding Kaspersky Lab represents only one instance of a much larger and very complicated cyber security challenge that the US government, many other governments, and private industry all face today. While I am indeed knowledgeable of Executive Order 13800 and the National Institute of Standards and Technology (NIST) Cybersecurity Framework, I will largely defer to my fellow witnesses who are in active government service to comment on the current implementation of those policy initiatives.

1.   Kaspersky Lab

In order to properly assess any risk posed by Kaspersky Lab products to the federal government, one must first understand the technical nature of those products themselves. As with many other ICT vendors and service providers, Kaspersky Lab remotely administers its services on client networks. Moreover, the very nature of Kaspersky Lab's security product offering is to provide constant and complete network monitoring to prevent and/or detect cyber intrusions and the harmful effects of malicious software. Discussions regarding the potential to introduce surreptitious "back doors" into Kaspersky Lab software are largely a moot point, because a well-known – and explicitly marketed feature -- of the product offering is a wide open "front door" for Kaspersky algorithms and technicians to not only view corporate network activity (including files and traffic flows) but also to issue remedial instructions to computers on the networks they protect.

An October 2014 marketing publication by Kaspersky Lab detailed the level of system monitoring that occurs:

> "Kaspersky System Watcher scans the most relevant system event data. The monitor tracks information about the creation and modification of files, the work of system services, any changes made to the system registry, system calls and data transfers over the network. System Watcher also processes information about operations with symbolic links containing references to files or directories, modifications of the master boot record where the loader for the installed operating system is stored and interception of OS boots. Moreover, it analyses the contents of the packets transmitted via TCP, the main Internet transport layer protocol, in search of any evidence of criminal activity. The data collection process is automated and does not require user interaction."[1]

There can be no doubt that Kaspersky Lab products are thorough in their network monitoring. That is exactly what its customers are knowingly and willingly paying for, and that directly contributes to the commercial success of its business.

Another important consideration is Kaspersky Lab's ability to aggregate network information from a large and geographically diverse client base. Like other cyber security firms, cloud service providers, and telecommunications companies, Kaspersky Lab has broad visibility of activity on the Internet. As a result, it is able to detect trends and anomalies that could indicate malicious software tools, cyber intrusion efforts, and even espionage operations.[2] That capability becomes equivalent to a global cyber intelligence analysis capacity and would therefore be of high interest to many nation states. In fact, numerous press articles from October 2017 state that Israeli intelligence officers penetrated Kaspersky Lab and thereby detected Russian spying efforts that also exploited the company's access and databases.[3]

The next issue that must be considered in assessing any risk of Kaspersky Lab products to federal government systems is whether willful complicity with foreign intelligence or security services is required for such threats to manifest themselves. The answer there is a resounding "no." If the media reports mentioned above are accurate, then at least two foreign governments have already penetrated and leveraged Kaspersky Lab's cyber security products and/or international ICT network access. While the company may remain adamant that such exploitation has occurred unwittingly, the question of knowing complicity may actually be a secondary counter-intelligence concern that distracts somewhat from the underlying cyber risk concern. I respect that the United States, Israel, and other governments may be highly interested in determining if Kaspersky Lab, or any of its employees, are operating in league with the Russian intelligence and security services, but that is immaterial from a basic analytic viewpoint. If Russian operatives – or Israeli operatives for that matter – have been able to exploit Kaspersky Lab, then the answer to the question about risk to federal government systems becomes tautological. Then only remaining question then is whether Kaspersky Lab is more prone or susceptible to such activity than other cyber security vendors, for it is clear that foreign intelligence services are not limited to exploiting the products of companies originating from their own countries. National laws and regulations may, however, make it much easier for them to do so.

In the case of the Russian Federation, world-class intelligence capabilities combined with legally mandated telecommunications monitoring for law enforcement and national security purposes makes the threat very real. "Russian law gives Russia's security service, the FSB, the authority to use SORM ("System for Operative Investigative Activities") to collect, analyze, and store all data that [sic] transmitted or received on Russian networks, including calls, emails, website visits and credit card transactions. SORM has been in use since 1990 and collects both metadata and content."[4] Accordingly, any Kaspersky Lab data that electronically transits ICT networks within Russian jurisdiction could, at least theoretically, be subject to Russian government surveillance.

So once again, willful complicity may not be a required element of any foreign intelligence threat related to Kaspersky Lab. If Kaspersky Lab were required by law to render its source code to Russian authorities, or if Kaspersky Lab communications from its global operations were subject to SORM monitoring at transit points in the Russian Federation, then its mere compliance would provide Russian authorities a clear intelligence advantage. In many respects, the subject matter of this Hearing is similar to previous investigations of Chinese ICT vendors conducted by the House Permanent Select Committee on Intelligence.[5] That report concluded that, although it could not prove wrongdoing, "The investigation concludes that the risks associated with Huawei's and ZTE's provision of equipment to U.S. critical infrastructure could undermine core U.S. national-security interests." The analysis centered mainly on the <u>potential</u> for intelligence access to be derived through corporate products of foreign origin, and shifted the focus to the known espionage activities and likely intent of the foreign government. Accordingly, any discussion of Kaspersky Lab must appropriately acknowledge the Russian cyber threat.

2. <u>Russian Cyber Operations</u>

The Director of National Intelligence's (DNI) Worldwide Threat Assessment from May 2017, leaves no doubt that Russia remains one of the most capable cyber adversaries of the United States. His testimony before the Senate Select Committee on Intelligence stated:

> "Russia is a full-scope cyber actor that will remain a major threat to US Government, military, diplomatic, commercial, and critical infrastructure. Moscow has a highly advanced offensive cyber program, and in recent years, the Kremlin has assumed a more aggressive cyber posture. ... In some cases, Russian intelligence actors have masqueraded as third parties, hiding behind false online personas designed to cause the victim to misattribute the source of the attack. ... We assess that Russian cyber operations will continue to target the United States and its allies to gather intelligence, support Russian decision-making, conduct influence operations to support Russian military and political objectives, and prepare the cyber environment for future contingencies."[6]

Russian efforts to influence the 2016 presidential election in the United States are just the latest in a long history of Russian cyber operations. The DNI 's testimony also noted that "Outside the United

States, Russian actors have conducted damaging and disruptive cyber attacks, including on critical infrastructure networks."

If one considers Russia's intentions in cyberspace and conjoins it with the kind of information and access that could be derived from exploitation of Kaspersky Lab products and services, then the risk must be considered to be substantial. Finally, in order to determine the magnitude of that risk, one would need to look well beyond the source code of those Kaspersky products themselves. A thorough review of Russian intelligence operations, telecommunications surveillance laws, and decryption capabilities would be required, as well as a proper understanding of the Internet traffic routing patterns of Kaspersky corporate communications.

The risk associated with the Russian Federation's cyber activities must be imputed to any ICT systems or vendors over which that country's authorities are able to exercise control – wittingly or unwittingly. In this case, Kaspersky Lab's assertions that it does not collaborate with any intelligence or security services are not necessarily inconsistent with the fact that its networks could be nonetheless exploited by such services. In fact, the open source reporting previously mentioned in this Statement for the Record would seem to suggest that is a very real concern. Russian cyber operations targeting United States interests would likely leverage any avenue that could provide the desired access or information.

3. Strategic Risk Management

The final topic that I would like to concentrate on is strategic risk management of cyber threats. The greatest factor in deterring or preventing foreign cyber espionage and cyber attacks is improving the resilience of the United States' own ICT networks. That holds true for both public and private sector infrastructures. As I envision it, such resilience includes both (i) better cyber defenses to prevent intrusions, as well as (ii) alternative back-up systems to provide critical services when the primary ICT networks that we rely upon are degraded. Cost-saving measures and the convergence of ICT platforms in general (at the network, protocol, and device level) have dramatically reduced the redundancy that can provide continuity of service under adverse circumstances. Many single "points" of failure (to include persons, processes, software applications, hardware platforms, logical protocols, infrastructure nodes, etc.) are being created which threaten the robustness of the information resources that underpin the governments, industry, and the global economy.

Executive Order 13800 and the NIST Cybersecurity Framework are important steps to help safeguard critical information infrastructures. Furthermore, I believe that information security practitioners must repeatedly assess their own enterprise networks and determine not only what information assets they possess, but also, what entities might seek to compromise (e.g. steal, expose, disrupt, destroy) those assets. For entities like the United States government whose networks are obvious targets of interest for foreign cyber actors, it may be appropriate to institute profound measures that reduce potential foreign access. Banning Kaspersky Lab products from federal systems may be one such measure, just as banning Huawei from the United States' telecommunications backbone was also deemed a necessary national security precaution.

It must be noted, however, that any such decisions may produce a reciprocal backlash from foreign governments that would adversely impact the commercial opportunities of US companies. I consider that economic policy consideration to be analytically distinct from questions of systemic cyber risk, but I am well aware that it will necessarily be part of related policy discussions. ICT vendors from the United States have already been disadvantaged as a result of previous geo-political strife, and one can presume more instances in the future. Therefore, from a policy perspective, it might be preferable to regulate or legislate against the factors and/or features that give rise to any cyber risks that are deemed unacceptable. For example, instead of outlawing Kaspersky Lab products per se, one could imagine restrictions that proscribe products of any origin that transmit US government data overseas or which maintain unfettered remote access throughout entire networks. In this regard, limitations could be imposed analogous to those that have been applied to cases brought before the Committee on Foreign Investment in the United States (CFIUS).

In conclusion, I assess that the threat of foreign cyber exploitation of Kaspersky Lab products remains a sincere concern for US federal networks. That assessment, however, rests largely on the public record of third-party exploitation, Russia's known cyber practices vis-à-vis the United States, and the inherent nature of Kaspersky's technological offerings. Willful collaboration would be a further concern, but one that is not necessarily required to assess a substantial risk. Finally, I would strongly recommend an equally rigorous analysis of the security of all ICT products used in federal networks – regardless of the national origin of the vendor – for we know that intelligence operatives are criminals alike are highly opportunistic actors.

Once again, thank you for the opportunity to provide this public service.

Respectfully submitted by Sean Kanuck, Director for Future Conflict and Cyber Security, IISS-Americas.

---

[1] Kasperksy Lab, "Preventing emerging threats with Kaspersky System Watcher", October 2014.

[2] Kaspersky Lab, Press Release entitled "Kaspersky Lab Identifies Operation 'Red October,' and Advanced Cyber-Espionage Campaign Targeting Diplomatic and Government Institutions Worldwide", 14 January 2013; Kaspersky Lab, Press Release entitled "Equation Group: The Crown Creator of Cyber-Espionage", 16 February 2015.

[3] The New York Times, "How Israel Caught Russian Hackers Scouring the World for U.S. Secrets", 10 October 2017; The Washington Post, "Israel hacked Kaspersky, then tipped the NSA that its tools had been breached", 10 October 2017; The Guardian, "Israel hack uncovered Russian spies' use of Kaspersky in 2015, report says", 11 October 2017.

[4] Center for Strategic and International Studies, Reference Note on Russian Communications Surveillance, 18 April 2014.

[5] Chairman Mike Rogers and Ranking Member C.A. Dutch Ruppersberger of the Permanent Select Committee on Intelligence, "Investigative Report on the U.S. National Security Issues Posed by Chinese Telecommunications Companies Huawei and ZTE", 8 October 2012.

[6] Daniel R. Coats, Director of National Intelligence, Statement for the Record, Worldwide Threat Assessment of the US Intelligence Community, 11 May 2017.

<u>SEAN KANUCK</u>

Sean Kanuck is the Director of the Future Conflict and Cyber Security program at the International Institute for Strategic Studies. He has also received several international appointments, including: Chair of the Research Advisory Group for the Global Commission on the Stability of Cyberspace (Hague, Netherlands), Distinguished Visiting Fellow at Nanyang Technological University (Singapore), and Distinguished Fellow with the Observer Research Foundation (New Delhi, India).

From 2011-2016, Sean led cyber analysis for the US Intelligence Community as its first National Intelligence Officer for Cyber Issues. He came to the National Intelligence Council after a decade of experience with the Central Intelligence Agency's Information Operations Center, the White House National Security Council, and the United States delegation to the United Nations Group of Governmental Experts on international information security.

Prior to government service, Sean practiced law with Skadden Arps in New York City, where he specialized in mergers and acquisitions, corporate finance, and banking matters. Sean holds degrees from Harvard University (A.B., J.D.), the London School of Economics (M.Sc.), and the University of Oslo (LL.M.).

Chairman LAHOOD. Thank you, Mr. Kanuck, for your opening statement, and thank all the witnesses for your opening statement. We will begin the questioning part of the hearing today, and with that, the Chair recognizes himself for five minutes.

I'd like to start. After months of denying any improper activity, and Kaspersky has claimed that any allegation they're involved with cyber espionage or involved with the Russian government, they claim that's false allegations, and today there's an article by Reuters that came out this morning on the cusp of this hearing titled, "Kaspersky says it obtained suspected NSA hacking code from U.S. computer," and that article goes on to say, and Kaspersky Lab admits "that its security software had taken source code for a secret American hacking tool from a personal computer in the United States." And in fact, in this article, the company admits that it exfiltrated the code earlier than previously reported and that Kaspersky gained access in 2014, and I think that's troubling on a lot of levels.

Let me just start off with you, Mr. Norton. Should the federal government have known about this incident?

Mr. NORTON. Thank you for the question. You know, I think that we need to take into effect that there's kind of the military side of federal networks, the military networks, and then there's the civilian side of networks, and I think, you know, what we're seeing today is that it's been years of really underfunded networks where we haven't really had the capability or the staffing or the opportunity to really take a look, an internal look at, you know, what is on the network outside of kind of these kind of clean-up that's going on right now in terms of removing what's on there. So I think that, you know, we need to take into effect that we haven't really taken this issue seriously. The Executive Branch is just now looking at this in the last couple of years and so I think that it's obviously a big miss and there's been a lot of success in terms of foreign adversaries being able to infiltrate not only the DOD, DHS and other networks as well as civilian networks, and so I think that it's definitely an issue that it's important that it's being covered in this hearing and that it is something that we need to know going forward. However, you know, I think we just haven't had the capability in place over the last couple of years to even know what's there, and I think that's part of the trouble.

Chairman LAHOOD. And Mr. Norton, what are the consequences of this revelation?

Mr. NORTON. Well, I think what you're seeing today is the government essentially scrambling to fix this. I think the fact that Homeland Security Secretary had this public announcement of removing the software is really alarming in the sense that, you know, for it to raise to that level, for the Secretary to put out an immediate edict across the federal government, I think that is certainly troubling and that's something that it says that we're not where we need to be and we have a long way to go to get there in terms of securing out networks.

Chairman LAHOOD. And does it surprise you that Kaspersky has denied this all the way through until today?

Mr. NORTON. You know, I don't have access to all the intelligence. You know, I think that the issue is not only, you know,

Kaspersky but I think other, you know, possible intruders that are, you know, on the network that are there. So I think this is absolutely a global issue. I think that, you know, for DHS and other intelligence communities to probably share more would be a good thing so the general public has a sense of what this means and how it is impacting our networks, so I think it's important for them to tell us a little bit more so we know what's going on.

Chairman LaHood. Ms. Dodson, same question for you in terms of should the federal government have known about this incident and what are the consequences of this revelation?

Ms. Dodson. So from the NIST perspective, security controls that we provide through our guidelines and special publications provide guidance on how to set up security for networks and be able to take a look at those. But a second critical issue relates to supply chain, and that is the ability to understand your suppliers, the kinds of products and services that you have and that you're using in your systems. NIST has been working with the federal government and with industry to develop supply chain guidelines as part of the Framework for Improving Critical Infrastructure that can be used to give organizations a much better understanding of those suppliers so that they can have the trust and confidence that they need when they put these products and services on their networks.

Chairman LaHood. As a follow-up on that, can you—what confidence can you give us that the NSA, their ability to stay ahead of our adversaries on this issue?

Ms. Dodson. I can't speak for another organization such as——

Chairman LaHood. Do you have an opinion on that?

Ms. Dodson. The federal government as a whole is taking the threat issues very seriously across government and working with industry to set up information-sharing systems so that as threat issues come up we can act and respond quickly. We are all taking this kind of issue very, very seriously.

Chairman LaHood. Thank you.

I now yield to Mr. Beyer for his questions.

Mr. Beyer. Thank you, Mr. Chairman, very much.

Mr. Norton, thank you for bringing up the LPTA issue. I will just quote you quickly: "Many CIOs are forced to abide by the lowest price technically acceptable, LPTA standard, which often means they don't up with the best products." I couldn't agree more, and we have a bipartisan bill, Mark Meadows and I, which has been reported out of the Oversight and Government Reform Committee unanimously. So if you can help us get it on the House Floor, we can get it passed unanimously and send it over to the Senate and not tie the hands of our purchasing agents on lowest price rather than encouraging them to get the best value.

Mr. Kanuck, Ms. Dodson talked about the voluntary risk-based, flexible, repeatable and cost-effective approach of the NIST Framework. So that's for the federal government. At what point do we ever consider making it mandatory across the U.S. business community or mandatory for subcontractors of the federal government? When do we elevate it to just beyond where we are?

Mr. Kanuck. Currently, that is not the approach under law and regulation. Private-sector entities are left to their own corporate policies and hiring cybersecurity elements to assist them. As far as taking legislative or regulatory actions to mandate certain activities, that may be forthcoming in the future but I cannot speculate on that. What the NIST Framework does is, it provides a baseline for a lot of the private sector to emulate what the government is doing and is required as Ms. Dodson said. I think that is universally viewed as a positive. And the challenge remains, is the U.S. government going to force actions on the private sector, and there are pros and cons to that.

Mr. BEYER. One of the things we may think about is, do we begin with government contractors?

Mr. KANUCK. That is actually a very interesting point to start, and clearly in the defense industrial base that is done through the procurement power of requiring certain aspects of cybersecurity to be utilized or followed by entities that are contracting with the U.S. government, and there's been success with that model. So that may be a model to be extended beyond just the defense contracting community. I think that would be a wise option.

Mr. BEYER. Mr. Kanuck, you probably know what's been called the Gerasimov Doctrine, so I'll take a moment to explain to others who may not have read it.

In 2013, General Valery Gerasimov, Russia's Chief of the General Staff, or head of its military, published an article titled "The Value of Science is in the Foresight" in a weekly Russian trade paper in which he let out—laid out his theory of modern warfare. He blends tactics developed by the Soviets with strategic military thinking about total war, which looks much more like the hacking of an enemy's society than attacking it head on. He wrote, "The very rules of war have changed. The role of non-military means of achieving political and strategic goals have grown. In many cases, they have exceeded the power of the force of weapons and their effectiveness. All of this is supplemented by military means of a concealed character."

So Mr. Kanuck, do you believe that we're seeing the Gerasimov Doctrine in practice during this last election cycle, and what are they trying to achieve by engaging these aggressive assaults on our democracy?

Mr. KANUCK. Well, I think you're not only seeing it in the form of influence operations in recent democratic elections in the United States and/or France, I think you've also seen it conjoined with military operations in Crimea or Ukraine as well. The Russian Federation, as I alluded to in my written comments and my opening statement, is very active in the area of information operations beyond the simple layer of cyber or critical infrastructure issues that we tend to think about. They actually used the word "information confrontation" when discussing this issue, and that is a wholesale part of their strategic paradigm. You can read it in the open translations of their strategic doctrine from 2000 onwards, and as you articulated it, I would wholeheartedly concur that you are seeing that assault on the intellectual and media space of societies through cyber means. What they have found is the perfect tool set, whether it's social media, remote hacking, et cetera, to achieve their philosophical objective through that stated doctrine.

Mr. Beyer. Thank you. Quick question. You wrote that all similar companies, the antivirus, could be unwittingly exploited by third parties. How at risk are Norton and MacAfee of this, you know——

Mr. Kanuck. I am not——

Mr. Beyer. —especially when you talk about they create the open front door.

Mr. Kanuck. So I'm not prepared to talk critically about other companies besides Kaspersky today. I will say, though, that a proper review of the features of a lot of these security softwares would allow you to do a proper assessment, and quite frankly, in my experience, foreign intelligence actors and criminals alike, once they find out who has access to the network they seek access will attempt to derive ways to exploit that path in, and it's a matter of intent and resources. I do not believe there is any network or any product that is perfectly secure. It's all a risk management issue.

Chairman LaHood. Thank you, Mr. Beyer.

I now yield to Mr. Higgins for his questions.

Mr. Higgins. Thank you, Mr. Chairman. I ask unanimous consent to enter a letter from Mr. Troy Newman, a cybersecurity professional with whom I consulted, to the record.

Chairman LaHood. Without objection.

[The information appears in Appendix II]

Mr. Higgins. Thank you, Mr. Chairman.

Ms. Dodson, how long have you been a cybersecurity advisor for the United States government?

Ms. Dodson. I have worked at NIST since 1987, and I've been the Chief Cybersecurity Advisor for about four years.

Mr. Higgins. So you were in place in 2012?

Ms. Dodson. Yes.

Mr. Higgins. You mentioned in one of your responses that the U.S. government is taking cybersecurity and the realm of cyberattack very seriously. Were we taking it very seriously in 2012 when the State Department contracted with Kaspersky?

Ms. Dodson. The federal government has been working on issues related to supply chain for about seven years, and we continue to work on our guidelines there as the complexity of our systems continue to grow. There are challenges in understanding all that we have in our networks but it's necessary to do that, and our work with the Framework to improve critical infrastructure cybersecurity provided some opportunities to think about supply chain, to think about resiliency in our networks so that we can understand cyber threat and respond quickly to those.

Mr. Higgins. So in your opinion, the United States government was taking cybersecurity very seriously in 2012?

Ms. Dodson. I think NIST has been taking cybersecurity seriously——

Mr. Higgins. Very well.

Ms. Dodson. —for a very long time.

Mr. Higgins. Mr. Chairman, Kaspersky product has over 400 million users nationwide. It's widely known Kaspersky's ties to the FSB. That's the Federal Security Service, the Russian Federation. FSB is the main successor to the Soviet Union's former KGB. Kaspersky headquarters is headquartered in Moscow in the former

KGB headquarter buildings in Lubyanka Square, and yet in 2012, the United States State Department contracted with Kaspersky. I read from Mr. Newman's letter that I entered into the official record earlier. Many security software users believe that security software is akin to a shield, that this shield wards off would-be attackers. The reality is that security software is more similar to an inoculation, as Mr. Kanuck pointed out earlier. Security software resides deep inside the computers and infrastructure within the very most sensitive and secure areas. In order to install any effective security software, we must first expose the system, making all information vulnerable. The security software has full access to all input and output operations. Security software is fully imbedded in such a way that it has complete access to total—to the entire system.

Mr. Shive, you're familiar with the end-user license agreement for security?

Mr. SHIVE. Yes, I am.

Mr. HIGGINS. That's the part that most Americans when we purchase a cybersecurity product, it appears on the screen and it's a lot of language that we don't read, we just click "I agree." Is that correct?

Mr. SHIVE. Yes.

Mr. HIGGINS. The end-user license agreement for Kaspersky systems is governed by the laws of the United States or by the laws of the Russian Federation?

Mr. SHIVE. If they're doing business in the United States, it would be governed by the United States.

Mr. HIGGINS. The end-user license agreement for Kaspersky products, Mr. Chairman, according to my research, are governed by the laws of the Russian Federation. We have certainly begun recently taking cybersecurity very seriously, but I find it alarming that although it was rather well known within the cybersecurity realm that Kaspersky was—you know, posed a particular risk—we continued to do business with them until very recently.

Let me just ask quickly, Mr. Shive. Are U.S. government employees restricted from using Kaspersky products, devices, on their own at this time?

Mr. SHIVE. I can't speak for the entire government. TSA employees are not restricted.

Mr. HIGGINS. Are Kaspersky products still allowed to be purchased by U.S. government agencies outside or separate from the GSA contract process?

Mr. SHIVE. Not if they're going to comply with the Binding Operational Directive that DHS published.

Mr. HIGGINS. And my colleague asked earlier, are U.S. government contractors restricted from using Kaspersky products?

Mr. SHIVE. Yes, they are as a result of the Binding Operational Directive.

Mr. HIGGINS. Mr. Chairman, my time has expired. I thank you for your cooperation.

Chairman LAHOOD. Thank you, Mr. Higgins.

I now yield to Ms. Johnson for her questions.

Ms. JOHNSON. Thank you very much.

Mr. Kanuck, the Russians appear to have a very good understanding of ways that they can attempt to influence America's views on certain issues or disrupt democratic institutions. Social scientists are now working with journalists and technologists and others to help understand these techniques and to identify them in order to forewarn the public about the covert efforts that intentionally generate disinformation and fake news for political purpose. Do you believe a robust understanding of social science and investment in the area of research can be applied to helping to thwart these sort of disinformation influence campaigns in the future?

Mr. KANUCK. Absolutely. I think we would want a triumvirate of government initiative efforts to protect systems. I think we would want the corporations whose social media or other platforms are being exploited to join the effort to preserve the integrity of their own corporate interests and networks. And then finally, broader public awareness and education to appreciate the risk and to take measures to secure their own systems would all be beneficial.

Ms. JOHNSON. Are there technologies we might be able to invest in to get a better grasp on this?

Mr. KANUCK. Certainly. There are a number of different innovative proposals, some being offered in the social-media community, others in the block chain technology. I believe this Committee even had discussions of quantum computing and quantum cryptography recently. So there are a number of different innovative technologies which may offer some additional security solutions in the future, and I do hope that both government and private-sector initiatives pursue them because as of right now, it is incredibly difficult to detect and/or prevent the kind of influence operations which you were referring to.

Ms. JOHNSON. Thank you very much.

I yield back Mr. Chairman.

Chairman LaHOOD. Thank you, Ms. Johnson.

At this time I'll yield to Mr. Posey—no, he's not there. We'll go to Mr. Marshall, Dr. Marshall of Kansas.

Mr. MARSHALL. Thank you, Mr. Chairman.

I think I'll start with Ms. Shive. Mr. Shive, is there a problem with the Kaspersky software now? Is there really a problem with it?

Mr. SHIVE. So the GSA position for Kaspersky is, there was a problem with them being entered onto GSA schedules the way that they were entered onto GSA schedules, hence them being removed. GSA doesn't run Kaspersky products so we haven't done deep and rich analysis into the capabilities or technologies associated with that.

Mr. MARSHALL. Was or is the Kaspersky Lab a threat to national security?

Mr. SHIVE. I'm not in a position to answer that. Our partners at DHS felt there was something significant enough to bar use of Kaspersky in the——

Mr. MARSHALL. When do you think they first would have thought or been concerned, approximately?

Mr. SHIVE. Who is "they"?

Mr. MARSHALL. DHS is who you mentioned.

Mr. SHIVE. Right.

Mr. MARSHALL. Or GSA, either one.

Mr. SHIVE. So GSA became aware that there was some discussion about the risk associated with Kaspersky at the end of last year, and then as news came out, we did a couple of evaluations on the GSA internal enterprise. When we found that we weren't running Kaspersky internally, we did no further deep and rich analysis of the technology embedded within Kaspersky. DHS can speak to when they became aware of——

Mr. MARSHALL. Mr. Kanuck, our friends in Israel obviously go back to 2014, it looks like, with a concern about that. Is that accurate that the Israel government maybe alerted us in 2014 that there was a problem?

Mr. KANUCK. Given the unclassified nature of this hearing, I'm going to have to simply refer to the recent media discussions that I saw in the New York Times, Washington Post, and Guardian and others that took it back to 2015.

Mr. MARSHALL. Okay. Mr. Norton, when the government identifies a problem in this aspect, whose responsibility is it to fix something like this? Is it particular to the people that are running the software or this is a bigger problem, maybe more of a national-security problem? Whose responsibility is it to fix the problem?

Mr. NORTON. That's absolutely a national-security issue. I think that, you know, on paper it's the Department of Homeland Security's challenge for the civilian side of the networks to fix this problem and to alert their other federal partners. I think that DHS has been challenged essentially since day one to kind of work their way around the bureaucracy that we have.

Mr. MARSHALL. It looks like to me this probably has been going on for two or three years. Frankly, I'm embarrassed. I've helped run a hospital and as well as part of a bank. I've seen us take on all these IT problems over the past decade. Absolutely convinced that if Thursday morning this is presented to me and we weren't solving the problem by Friday that people would have been fired and lost their job over it, and this looks like to me it took three years when we knew there was a problem, a potential problem. Even if it was just a potential problem, if it's a national-security issue, we should have been fixing it yesterday, not tomorrow. Am I—what's wrong with my expectations, Mr. Norton?

Mr. NORTON. I think your expectations are absolutely fair and they're right on, and I think that the government has——

Mr. MARSHALL. Mr. Kanuck, are my expectations unrealistic?

Mr. KANUCK. I think the desire to remediate things as soon as possible is very well placed. I'm also aware that the speed of changes in government can occasionally be slow.

Mr. MARSHALL. Okay. You know, I think of this concept of the fox and the henhouse. Again, I go back to my experience working with a hospital and bank. If we would have vendors applying to do our IT and to protect our stuff, and if I would have brought to the board people with connections to the Russian government, A, they would have probably fired me, and B, they would have fired the IT person who even let them in the door. I mean, did this pass the sniff test, Mr. Kanuck? Would they pass the sniff test today to get this type of contract?

Mr. KANUCK. If it's meant to protect the information of a sensitive national security type, I would think that it would not pass the sniff test because of the foreign penetrations and foreign influence that we have previously discussed here.

Mr. MARSHALL. Mr. Shive, in today's environment, would they pass—the smell test is a better term. I've been corrected by my colleagues across the aisle. We called it sniff in Kansas. Maybe it's smell other——

Mr. SHIVE. Again, because we don't run that particular software, I can't say specifically, and we don't base those evaluations on press reports. What I can say is that every agency CIO has a responsibility and obligation to vet any software or technology or process that runs in that organization, and that if Kaspersky or any similar tool was going to be entered into service in that agency, it would be put through a battery of tests to evaluate whether or not it was suitable for that environment.

Mr. MARSHALL. Mr. Chairman, may I have 30 more seconds?

Chairman LaHOOD. I'll yield you 30 more seconds.

Mr. MARSHALL. You know, it feels like with all these IT issues that we have, people are trying to rob the bank, and as long as they don't get—as long as they don't rob the bank, we don't prosecute them. What do we do when people are just trying to rob the bank? So all these attacks on us, people are trying to rob the bank. They're trying to rob us of information? What's the solution to trying to—I mean, my gosh, I can't believe this goes on this much. They're robbing—they're trying to rob the bank, they don't accomplish it, so it seems like nothing happens to them. Does anybody have a solution, a short solution? Mr. Kanuck, you raised your hand.

Mr. KANUCK. Where we lack the ability to have cooperative international law enforcement or forensic capabilities to identify and prosecute those individuals, we are left with recourse to improving our own networks' resiliency.

Mr. MARSHALL. Thank you. I yield back.

Chairman LaHOOD. Thank you, Dr. Marshall.

I now yield to Mr. McNerney.

Mr. McNERNEY. I thank the Chairman. I thank the witnesses. It's certainly an important subject and I want to pursue a little bit.

Mr. Norton, in your written testimony, you mentioned that budget cuts across the federal government are affecting—are forcing federal officials to use the lowest price technically available standards. What aspects of security might be compromised as a result of that lowering of standards?

Mr. NORTON. Well, I think that, you know, sequestration, which was put in place 7 or eight years ago, right now what we're seeing is the impacts of sequestration where we've essentially conditioned government executives, CIOs, other managers to really look for that LPTA product and they might not necessarily look for the best type of software that's available, maybe something that's customized, something that might fit the particular need of an agency, and also we're seeing where they're not turning on the software to fully capability and that they maybe use part of an acquisition and maybe not all of it and so I think all that goes to not having enough resources and being kind of constrained to the sequestration that's essentially still in place and kind of hovering——

Mr. MCNERNEY. Are there specific examples you could submit to the Committee of this phenomenon you're describing?

Mr. NORTON. I think that broadly I would say, you know, program to program from, you know, federal agencies, you know, like at DHS where they have, you know, component agencies like Customs and Border Protection or other places where, you know, you've got components that are purchased that might not necessarily have a cyber component, you know, put inside of it.

I think if you think about the commercial attack back in October of last year where essentially the internet was slowed down because they were attacking a piece of the internet from a small company in, you know, New Hampshire. You find these little parts that can be exploited and slow down the internet overall, and you think of that broadly in terms of other products that maybe are purchased day to day at, you know, Best Buy, for example, that don't necessarily have cyber built into it goes to that lowest price technically acceptable.

Mr. MCNERNEY. Thank you.

Mr. Shive, are commercial antivirus computer security software products made by other companies also potentially vulnerable to the same sorts of exploitation as in the case of Kaspersky?

Mr. SHIVE. Because of the persistent nature of the threat, all softwares are vulnerable, and that's why CIOs have the obligation to assess those softwares before they enter them into service in each of their agencies.

Mr. MCNERNEY. Do you have any recommendations for federal— to protect federal systems?

Mr. SHIVE. Increased investment in cybersecurity is a very good idea.

Mr. MCNERNEY. Ms. Dodson, has NIST made available any guidelines or best practices concerning security of voting infrastructure?

Ms. DODSON. NIST has developed guidelines for voting infrastructures that relate to cybersecurity and in particular looking at risk-management processes that can be put in place for the different phases of voting systems and voting use.

Mr. MCNERNEY. Should NIST be doing more in this arena?

Ms. DODSON. NIST is continuing to work with the voting community as well as the Department of Homeland Security as they are also looking at security and voting systems, so we are continuing our efforts there.

Mr. MCNERNEY. Okay. What limitation's do you face?

Ms. DODSON. I'm sorry. What kind of limitation do we face in——

Mr. MCNERNEY. Right.

Ms. DODSON. So NIST continues to look at a number of different aspects of voting and work with that community. We are looking at security. We are looking at the interoperability and the usability, so many different aspects of voting systems to support the United States and to support the different states as they're developing and implementing their solutions.

Mr. McNerney. Thank you. Mr. Shive, what would you recommend small businesses do to strengthen their cybersecurity networks and practices?

Mr. Shive. For small businesses, employ the best practices that exist for large business and government in their cybersecurity practices, make an emphasis and focus on cybersecurity from the ground up at the beginning of creation of their product, tools, process or service rather than as a bolt on at the end.

Mr. McNerney. But a lot of these small businesses don't have the resources to have an IT person to take care of those issues.

Mr. Shive. And then they'll suffer the same fate that every other corporation that makes that fundamental mistake does and they'll go out of business.

Mr. McNerney. Thank you. Mr. Chairman, I yield back.

Chairman LaHood. Thank you, Mr. McNerney.

I now yield to the gentleman from South Carolina, Mr. Norman.

Mr. Norman. Thank you, Mr. Chairman.

Mr. Shive, when we talk about getting on the GSA's preapproved contract list, who's got the final approval? Is it a person, is it a group? Who would make the final call on that?

Mr. Shive. The Federal Acquisition Service in GSA, which is made up of contracting officers, lawyers, and business professionals who interact with the vendor community and create a framework for their entrance into the schedules.

Mr. Norman. How many people is that?

Mr. Shive. I can get back to you with the number. I think it's around 6,000 people.

Mr. Norman. Okay. Now, was Congressman Higgins right when he mentioned the fine print of being under the—and I forget which agency he mentioned but being under the, I guess the legal guidelines of Soviet Union rather than the United States? Is that right?

Mr. Shive. So thank you for asking that clarifying question. So every company has a EULA as a part of their business practice. The federal government, the U.S. federal government is not obligated under that EULA to enter service. There's a negotiation that takes place that includes on the government side lawyers and contracting officers that assess the EULA relative to the regulation and policy of the federal government. If there's a disconnect there, then the vendor can't do business with government.

Mr. Norman. Okay. So going forward, would that be—would any changes be made on that?

Mr. Shive. No. I think it's a good process to have government lawyers and contracting officers scanning that test for corporations and making sure that it complies with federal regulation and law.

Mr. Norman. Okay. And Mr. Shive, in your testimony you note that three resellers included Kaspersky's products without taking appropriate steps to modify the contracts. Is that right?

Mr. Shive. That's right.

Mr. Norman. Did these three resellers comply with the GSA's request to remove Kaspersky products from the list?

Mr. Shive. Yes, they did so immediately.

Mr. Norman. After the fact?

Mr. Shive. Yes.

Mr. NORMAN. Okay. Did the GSA evaluate whether these three resellers needed to be sanctioned for including the products?

Mr. SHIVE. I'm not aware of the sanctioning process, of any sanctioning process.

Mr. NORMAN. Do you think there need to be sanctions, at least go down—to go down that path to have consequences? Because it looks like just from what I'm hearing has really been the—there's no consequences on this.

Mr. SHIVE. Right. So I'm actually not saying that there were or were not consequences. I just don't know if there was. We can circle back to you and get you that information.

Mr. NORMAN. Like Congressman Marshall mentioned, you know, the consequences in the private sector, the consequences in just about everything in the political arena, and it looks like there ought to be consequences with this. It's pretty serious from what I'm hearing today.

Mr. SHIVE. Understood. We're happy to circle back with you and let you know what the consequences were, if there were in fact any.

Mr. NORMAN. Thanks so much.

I yield back, Mr. Chairman.

Chairman LAHOOD. Thank you, Mr. Norman.

I now will yield to Mr. Perlmutter from Colorado.

Mr. PERLMUTTER. I thank the Chair, and just an inquiry of the Chair. Was Mr. Kaspersky invited to testify or somebody from his organization?

Chairman LAHOOD. Not to today's hearing. I know that we plan to have a few more hearings on this, and we'll entertain that as we move along.

Mr. PERLMUTTER. All right. Thank you.

And Mr. Norton, it's good to see you. We've had two records today. You have had the shortest opening statement, and the Ranking Member had the shortest questioning along with Mr. Norman today that we've had I think on this Committee of all time, so thank you all.

You know, over time the computers I've had, I've had MacAfee, I've had Kaspersky, and I've had—and Mr. Norton, I don't think it's your company but I've had Norton antivirus too.

Mr. NORTON. It is not my company.

Mr. PERLMUTTER. I think this is a very important hearing we're having today. Mr. Higgins talked about the KGB potentially having access into governmental records, talked about—I think Dr. Marshall talked about the fox in the henhouse and robbing the bank or attempting to rob the bank, and words like "trusted" and "complicit" and "willful" and "adversarial" and "espionage" and "intelligence risk" and "national security" have been bandied about today. What—I'll start with you, Mr. Kanuck. What is it that we're worried about here?

Mr. KANUCK. I believe we're particularly worried about the ability for unauthorized users to access systems and either steal confidential information or disrupt the availability of——

Mr. PERLMUTTER. But a particular unauthorized user, who is that? What is that?

Mr. KANUCK. Well, from my role as a Strategic Threat Analyst, I would say there are numerous of them in the international space.

The one we seem to be focusing on today is the Russian threat actor and that has theoretically, according to open-source reporting, exploited Kaspersky products to that end.

Mr. PERLMUTTER. Mr. Norton, are you familiar with Guccifer 2.0?

Mr. NORTON. Yes.

Mr. PERLMUTTER. What is that?

Mr. NORTON. Well, essentially it's hacktivism, if you will, in terms of, you know, hacking into, finding information, you know, getting into a system and then pulling information out. I think your assessment in terms of what exactly we're talking about here is a great point. I think there are multiple threats. Whether they're here domestically or they're international, I think the government is woefully behind in terms of preparation in terms of what we've done now and what we need to do, you know, going forward. I think that we seem to be having, you know, these type of discussions every 6 to 12 months with these massive hacks that are occurring, and I think that, you know, it's time to really kind of move on and figure out what is the next step, whether it's massive research and development funding for the government to hire these, you know, more experts, bring people in to government. I think that we've, you know, kind of assigned this opportunity to CIOs and other people within the government that have had traditional roles and now they seem to be the cybersecurity experts, and I think they obviously do a great job for us but I also think they need more help and more services and more, you know, support.

Mr. PERLMUTTER. And the Congress has got to be in the lead hopefully of providing those resources, which I think you now mentioned and Mr. Kanuck mentioned.

So let me move to NIST and to the GSA for just a second and then I've got a political statement I want to make. I think one of the places where we can harden systems especially for small business is through small business taking advantage of the NIST Framework and that the GSA in its protocols demand that small business have access, you know, taking advantage of those NIST protocols or Framework, just if the two of you would comment real quickly.

Ms. DODSON. NIST has developed some guidance specifically for small businesses around the Framework to make that publicly available, and we've worked with the Small Business Administration, with our manufacturing Extension Partnership and others to make sure these guidelines are available and that small businesses can find out about them.

Mr. PERLMUTTER. But for you, they're guidelines. For GSA, they could demand something like that as part of the purchase.

Mr. SHIVE. And that's exactly right. Increasingly we find that business both big and small is increasingly availing themselves of NIST policy, guide work and frameworks because it's good IT and cybersecurity practice. As a CIO who purchases softwares and technologies increasingly I'm asking my vendor partners to conform to those standards as well.

Mr. PERLMUTTER. If I could have just a few more seconds, Mr. Chairman——

Chairman LaHOOD. Absolutely.

Mr. PERLMUTTER. —for my political statement?

Chairman LaHood. It depends on what it is but——

Mr. Perlmutter. Well, you're not going to like it but I mean, I think this is a very important subject but obviously, you know, when we have at the White House an investigation between connections between the White House and many of its people with the guy who was the former head of the KGB, Vladimir Putin, then we've got a lot of ground to cover, whether it's within the cybersecurity or as to, you know, just basic oldpersonal relationships and not have too many front doors to Russia because I think that is jeopardizing our national security, and with that, I yield back.

Chairman LaHood. Thank you, Mr. Perlmutter.

At this time I'll yield to Mr. Loudermilk of Georgia.

Mr. Loudermilk. Thank you, Mr. Chairman, and thank all of you for being here today.

Spending 20 years in the IT industry, actually 30 if you include my time in the intelligence community when I was in the military, there are so many aspects of this issue that are so disturbing that I can't even get my hands around all of it, and some of it outside of this hearing such as an intelligence analyst taking classified material home. I mean, that was a felony when I was in the intelligence community. And then somebody who is in that arena having pirated software, I mean, anybody who works in this arena at all, you know that if it's pirated software, it's dirty. It's likely dirty in some way. So anyhow, that's outside the scope of this. This happened in a previous Administration and hopefully we're cleaning up some of the looseness that we've had in the intelligence community, but I'm reading an article from Associated Press which, Mr. Chairman, I'd like to introduce into the record.

Chairman LaHood. Without objection.

[The information appears in Appendix II]

Mr. Loudermilk. This thing reads like a Clancy novel, the Israelis spying on the Russians who are spying on us, and they alert us to the fact that the Russians are gaining information that are being captured through this software.

Mr. Norton, in your experience, if a cybersecurity company comes across, whether intentional or unintentional, comes across classified information, I would think, through my experience, that it not only legally but professionally you should alert the agency of which it came from that—or at least the proper officials that you have come across this information. Am I wrong in that? Is that something that you would assess if somebody just happened to come across this information they would alert?

Mr. Norton. I think in the last couple of years that there has been an effort in terms of sharing information amongst DHS and other, you know, companies across the cyber realm, if you will, in terms of moving information back and forth certainly could be better but I think the process has started and I think as you're seeing professionals kind of cross into the private sector and back into government and back and forth, it's getting a little bit better, but absolutely, it's something that we need to continue to get our arms around and do a better job.

Mr. Loudermilk. I mean, if in your business you come across a piece of classified information that was not within your realm of need to know, you would report to someone?

Mr. NORTON. Of course.

Mr. LOUDERMILK. Okay. In this article from Associated Press, you know, they reported that Israel notified us that Russia was gaining classified information using the software. Eugene Kaspersky spoke—in this article, he stated that they did collect NSA materials clearly marked classified in 2014, which were spirited to Moscow for analysis, and then deleted at his direction. When asked if Kaspersky alerted the NSA that his software discovered classified materials, he claimed that he didn't want to see it in the news. If he is asked why he didn't report it, he didn't want to see in the news that I tried to contact the NSA to report the case, definitely I didn't want to see it in the news. Is that plausible that he would not report that they, you know, came across by unintentional means that they came across classified information? Is it plausible that he would have not reported it just because he didn't want to see it in the news? Yes, Mr. Norton. I'm sorry.

Mr. NORTON. I guess the answer is, sir, I don't know what's going inside his head or what his thought process was. It's hard for me to assess why he made that decision or didn't make that decision.

Mr. LOUDERMILK. To me, from a legal aspect, maybe laws have changed since I was in the intelligence community but I would have a legal responsibility at that point to notify the authorities look, our software came across this information, you may need to go look at this employee. I also have issue with them just reading the documents they come across as well.

Mr. Kanuck, do you think this is a plausible response by Mr. Kaspersky?

Mr. KANUCK. My first observation would be that Mr. Kaspersky may not be subject to a secrecy agreement of any kind that would have the legal contractual binding nature that yourself previously and myself have had before that would have obligated us to report that information had we stumbled across it. Secondly, I guess I am personally a little surprised that knowing the scrutiny that his firm is under that he might not have taken an opportunity to return it to the U.S. government and try to get in our good favor.

Mr. LOUDERMILK. Maybe redeem himself, you know, to show goodwill.

Let me ask you, why would he not inform the NSA? I mean——

Mr. KANUCK. Possibly because he felt there was no legal obligation for him to, and in his personal decision thought it was not in the best interest of his company, which again is a Russian company.

Mr. LOUDERMILK. Mr. Norton, is it plausible that maybe the suspicions that the Israelis have, that we have is that they're purposely mining for information? Is that plausible?

Mr. NORTON. I think that, you know, with the digital age having really grown in the last 15 years that online intelligence gathering is the normal. I think that we as, you know, society need to continue to come to grips with the fact that mining online data and the fact that you can target individuals is the new normal and that we all need to be aware of this, and I think that whether it's the Russians or other adversaries, nation-states, individuals, absolutely our networks are a target every day, every second, and we need to be really aware of that.

Mr. LOUDERMILK. Why would be send it to Moscow? Is that not suspect that he sent the documents to Moscow, then asked for them to be deleted, Mr. Norton?

Mr. NORTON. I think—again, I don't know what really occurred or didn't occur. It seems like that would be something that we would need to really kind of take a look at, and hopefully our intelligence services is on that and they can give us——

Mr. LOUDERMILK. Mr. Kanuck, would you—would you find it suspect that he sends them to Moscow after seeing that they're classified NSA documents determines to not notify the NSA but then sends them to Moscow and then says I'm going to have them deleted? I mean, that's pretty suspect to me.

Mr. KANUCK. So again, I'm not personally knowledgeable of whether he himself was the one who did the discovering and the forwarding. I would, as I said in my opening statement, encourage the analysis of traffic flows within the Kaspersky global communications network. That may have been standard operating procedure or it may have been an ad hoc decision. I can't speak to that because I don't work for that company.

Mr. LOUDERMILK. All right. Well, thank you, Mr. Chairman. I yield back the time I have exceeded.

Chairman LaHood. Well, thank you, Mr. Loudermilk, for your insightful questions there.

That concludes our questions here today. I want to thank the witnesses for your valuable testimony here today. I think this Committee as part of our oversight mission will continue to investigate leads and evidence as it relates to this matter. Secondly, I think we've just touched the surface as it relates to Kaspersky and their alleged complicity and involvement with cyber espionage, and this Committee will continue to work on that. We anticipate more hearings and more testimony to come.

So with that, this hearing is concluded, and we thank you.

[Whereupon, at 11:31 a.m., the Subcommittee was adjourned.]

Appendix I

Answers to Post-Hearing Questions

Responses by Mr. Sean Kanuck

RESPONSES TO QUESTIONS FOR THE RECORD
As Submitted by Rep. Eddie Bernice Johnson

by

Sean Kanuck
Director for Future Conflict and Cyber Security
IISS-Americas

for

United States House of Representatives
Committee on Science, Space, and Technology
Subcommittee on Oversight

Hearing entitled
"Bolstering the Government's Cybersecurity: Assessing the Risk of
Kaspersky Lab Products to the Federal Government"

held on
25 October 2017

Chairman LaHood, Ranking Member Beyer, and distinguished Members of Congress:

Thank you again for the invitation to testify before the Subcommittee on Oversight during its hearing on 25 October 2017. I am also pleased to take this opportunity to respond to the questions for the record submitted by Ranking Member Eddie Bernice Johnson of the Committee on Science, Space, and Technology. Several of her questions referred to statements I made in my op-ed entitled "Get ready for Democracy 3.0" that was published in The Hill on the same day as the hearing, so I respectfully request to incorporate that piece by reference rather than reiterating the full content in its entirety here.

Question 1.a In what ways have Russia's influence operations become more effective?

In the last two years, Russian influence operations have become both more brazen and more effective from a Western political perspective. Allegations of Russian (dis)information campaigns related to the "Brexit" vote, the US presidential election, the French presidential election, and the Catalan independence referendum, suggest an increasing level of intervention in countries beyond Russia's historical sphere of influence (i.e. the former Soviet Union and Eastern Europe).[1] Russian activities have leveraged existing political strife in the United States and Europe to foment discord and raise questions regarding the fundamental institutions of liberal democracy, namely the legitimacy of elections and the rule of law. Creating such uncertainties has a destabilizing effect on Russia's competitors – which must now focus more political energy on domestic concerns in lieu of checking Moscow's foreign policy moves on the global stage – and provides a public relations advantage among the Kremlin's own domestic audience. Russian influence operations have become more effective because they have now challenged the basic assumptions about democratic government and liberal values in an open society. The ongoing congressional hearings, media coverage, and popular discourse are all a testament to the success of Moscow's recent influence campaigns.

Moreover, that approach is consistent with Russia's views on information conflict as well as its stated military doctrine. According to paragraph 23 of the 2016 Doctrine of Information Security of the Russian Federation, the main thrusts of information security include *inter alia* "suppressing the activity detrimental to the national security of the Russian Federation", "improving information support activities to implement the State policy of the Russian Federation", and "neutralizing the information impact intended to erode Russia's traditional moral and spiritual values."[2] In 2012, Russia's Chief of General Staff, Nikolai Marakov, even commented on the military's role in "working on domestic and foreign public opinion using the media, Internet and more."[3]

Question 1.b What about the "scale and scope" has changed?

Several quantitative and qualitative factors have contributed to the higher effectiveness of influence operations conducted via cyberspace. First, automated technologies permit fewer operators to both monitor and/or produce data flows on a greater scale. That means fewer working hours are required to generate impact, because "botnets" and "astroturfing" (i.e. the fabrication of seemingly "grass-roots" support on social media) can multiply the perceived popularity of ideas (e.g. "trending"). In essence, a number of strategically placed advertisements and social media postings that are then (inadvertently) promulgated by other Internet platforms and large search engines can have a disproportionate impact. Second, the geographic reach – or scope – of influence operations has almost no limit. Individuals from Moscow, St. Petersburg, or anywhere else can induce their desired effects in nearly any country around the world over the Internet. That is especially true in liberal democracies which pride themselves on freedom of expression, an open press, and little or no online censorship. Operatives no longer need to be physically resident in – or within radio communication distance of – the jurisdiction they wish to influence.

Those quantitative changes dramatically alter the qualitative calculus for conducting such influence operations. Cyber-enabled influence operations are fairly costless and potentially quite effective compared to other foreign policy options. There is little or no physical risk to the operators themselves, and precedents to date show only minimal repercussions for their state sponsors if the activities are ever attributed to them.

Question 1.c Finally, what specific new tools have Russian Intelligence leveraged in their more effective campaigns in the U.S. and elsewhere, and how have they used these tools?

The 2017 US Intelligence Community Assessment entitled "Assessing Russian Activities and Intentions in Recent US Elections" concluded that Russia's messaging strategy blended "covert intelligence operations—such as cyber activity—with overt efforts by Russian Government agencies, state-funded media, third-party intermediaries, and paid social media users or 'trolls.'"[4] That report also indicated that Russian military intelligence publicized material online, directly or indirectly, through Guccifer 2.0., DCLeaks.com, media outlets, and WikiLeaks.[5] Moscow used both new tools (e.g. computer hacking, social media, Internet websites) and traditional methods (e.g. espionage, broadcast television). It is noteworthy that these various tools were used in concert in order to create a combined, strategic effect. Perhaps the most important lesson learned is that a series of coordinated propaganda activities can produce a much greater impact today than in previous eras. That is the political analogue of "cross-channel" or "multi-channel" marketing in the business environment.

Social media played a significant role in recent Russian influence campaigns. Facebook has acknowledged that Russia was linked to thousands of political advertisements on its platform.[6] Twitter also had numerous Russian-linked accounts; furthermore, its platform enabled large-scale, automated messaging that could be conducted by a relatively small number of individuals.[7] These tools, and others, were used to create the impression that Americans were responsible for the views being represented and that certain ideas had much broader support than they did in reality – thereby skewing the discourse towards foreign-generated, extreme, and/or minority viewpoints. It also fueled partisanship and distrust in the electoral system.

Question 2.a How did Russian intelligence use social media in its efforts to influence the 2016 Presidential Election?

This response builds on my answer to Question 1.c above. Russia used "trolls" (i.e. paid social media participants) to post and "tweet" about particular issues. These agents were instructed to propagate certain memes and spread discontent regarding controversial topics such as racism, police violence, gun control, and gender/sexual orientation.[8] For example, Facebook (unwittingly) sold $100,000 in advertisements to a pro-Kremlin "troll farm."[9] Using automated botnets, Russian actors could then "re-tweet" or "like" those original (or other selected) social media posts and advertisements to increase their perceived popularity. Those memes that "trended" in social media were then picked up by search engines and other news outlets. As a result, postings from relatively obscure origins – some completely false – captured the attention of "mainstream" political discussions.

In addition, Russian influence operations were explicitly designed to exacerbate existing political rifts, in some cases promulgating views on both sides of highly divisive issues.[10] The strategic objective of Russian intelligence was to destabilize and/or discredit the US electoral process, not just to favor any specific candidate. Russia's intervention was not simply about Trump or Clinton; it was about trust in government institutions, international reputation, global politics, and "soft power" projection.

Question 2.b How would you attempt to identify and limit foreign interventions in our democracy while upholding our basic democratic principles and institutions, including a free press?

Finding an operative solution to the problems identified above is no easy task. To a certain extent, the national interest in the security and fidelity of elections is somewhat at odds with the national interest in freedom of expression. In reality, neither value can be enjoyed in its fullest extreme if both are to be enjoyed. A second critical factor is that the social media platforms in question are private companies not government agencies. Accordingly, efforts to limit such foreign interventions will either need to be done consensually by those firms or else be imposed through regulation.

Restricting the almost unlimited freedom of expression over social media (whether done by government or the private sector) in order to safeguard democratic principles may seem paradoxical, but that is essentially what would be required to identify and limit foreign interventions. If I understand the concerns over Russia's influence operations correctly, they are twofold: (A) the actors were foreign, and (B) they achieved a disproportionate impact. There are three possible parameters for limiting intervention – content, origin, and propagation – and each merits closer consideration.

First, content-based restrictions for social media would be antithetical to the First Amendment to the US Constitution and the desired objective of open political discourse surrounding elections. Therefore, I would personally limit any such restrictions to the general legal prohibitions against the incitement to violence or threats to public safety.

Second, freedom of expression does not necessarily imply complete freedom of anonymous expression. A free press need not be an anonymous press; however, anonymity has historically been a safeguard against persecution. Requiring social media companies to disclose the source of political advertisements or the provenance of memes could be difficult and costly. But, that would be the only way to address concern (A) regarding foreign voices manipulating the US political discourse surrounding elections. While I would personally favor such disclosure for online political campaigns, I must acknowledge that the majority of politically-infused speech on social media would not meet the criteria of an explicit campaign advertisement. Regulatory efforts to demarcate between election-related speech whose speaker must be identified and general social media content which could remain anonymous would be onerous if not downright infeasible. Simple disclosure of paid advertising sponsors and/or foreign-registered user accounts might be practical, intermediate steps.

Third, US campaign finance laws currently try to limit the disproportionate impact of individual entities by placing limits on donations (and disclosing the identity of donors). A similar effort to mitigate concern (B) above could conceivably be applied to social media activity concerning elections. Although I am aware that some countries limit expenditures on and/or provide egalitarian access to broadcast media for election campaigns,[11] I believe it would be impracticable to apply such approaches in the context of social media and the propagation of memes. The number of online fora, the number of user accounts, and the sheer volume of posts (and re-posts or links) would make such regulation unduly burdensome. Precluding disproportionate impact would also presuppose the ability to identify the origin of the activity, which reverts to concern (A) above.

In summary, I offer that disclosure of foreign paid advertisements and foreign-registered social media accounts would be the least intrusive, and probably the only feasible, way to identify and limit foreign interventions. That would, however, require social media companies to "know their customer" in a way that would remove anonymity from the social media environment.

Question 3.a Do you have any recommendations regarding what the federal, state or local governments can do to ensure our election/voting infrastructure is well protected from potential cyber attacks?

As with any other critical infrastructure, the resiliency of the election/voting infrastructure consists of strong defenses to prevent compromises as well as intentional redundancy to overcome any compromises or occasional degradations. Recent studies have shown the vulnerabilities of electronic voting machines,[12] and nearly all – if not all – Internet-accessible computer systems are currently susceptible to remote hacking. Therefore, I offer the following ten recommendations:

(1) Subject all electronic voting machine hardware and software to rigorous "red teaming" (i.e. penetration testing) by offensive experts from the government and private sector.
(2) Harden voting machines against all electromagnetic transmissions.
(3) Conduct tests of electronic voting machines with sample sizes equal to election-day turnouts and on the same calendar date (i.e. internal clock setting) as the election itself.
(4) Properly vet all polling station personnel who will have physical access to voting machines. (This also applies to access to any storage facilities between elections.)
(5) Predicate any future online or wireless voting capabilities upon biometric verification.
(6) Fund research and development of advanced technologies (e.g. blockchain, quantum cryptography, etc.) for establishing secure, online elections in the future.
(7) Maintain all original paper ballots indefinitely for audit purposes.
(8) Conduct random audits of paper ballots to verify electronic vote tallies as well as mandatory audits of paper ballots for precinct results within a specified margin of error.
(9) Provide an opt-in capability for voters to verify if their own votes were recorded accurately. (Many voters may prefer this option to an uncertain secret ballot.)
(10) Apply machine learning algorithms to detect statistical anomalies for further investigation (cf. insider trading and credit card or telecommunications billing fraud.)

Voting is the essential "transaction" of democracy and the integrity of that process needs to be protected as much if not more than any other financial or economic transaction. My recommendations (1) through (4) above involve improving the defenses of existing voting systems. Recommendations (5) and (6) speak to developing better systems for the future. Finally, recommendations (7) through (10) are intended to provide an *ex post* "check sum" on the system to guarantee its results are valid.

Question 3.b Do you have any recommendations regarding efforts the U.S. government, state or local governments or others, should take to help identify foreign influence operations against the United States?

This response builds on my answer to Question 2.b above. It may be appropriate for the federal or state governments to require disclosure of paid advertising sponsors or foreign-registered social media accounts in certain contexts that affect domestic elections, but I would strive to keep such regulation to a minimum. Social media has proven to be a powerful tool for popular discourse that has empowered individuals from all backgrounds and socio-economic strata to voice their opinions. I firmly believe that the United States is unique – and better off – for maintaining its open political dialogue about all issues, including with foreign contributions that are intended to inform or engage Americans (vice misinform, purely promote controversy, or falsely distort elections). It is undeniable that French political philosophy contributed to the drafting of the US Constitution and that Britain's abolition of slavery further encouraged the same in the United States.

It is most apposite to conclude with a discussion of the private companies that operate the social media platforms and search engines. Facebook, Twitter, Instagram, Google, etc. are best placed to detect and interdict foreign efforts to manipulate their own networks; moreover, the events of 2016 and 2017 have not only raised their awareness of foreign interventions but also shown the deleterious effects that influence operations can have on their business reputation. Those companies already employ advanced machine learning algorithms for search optimization, facial recognition, and other business purposes, so it would not be unreasonable for them apply similar techniques to detect illegal, fraudulent, and/or foreign activity on their networks. In fact, companies like Facebook and Twitter have increasingly been removing terrorist and hate speech accounts.[13]

In many respects, the private business interests of those companies will actually be aligned with the objectives of the governmental authorities seeking to protect the integrity of electoral processes. Social media firms do not want to be unwittingly manipulated by foreign interest groups (or domestic ones for that matter), and the nominal advertising revenue to be gained from a foreign intelligence service's covert influence campaign would not justify jeopardizing a corporate brand worth billions of dollars. Therefore, I would recommend minimalist regulatory approaches that leverage those common interests and make the implementation of any "know your customer" and/or disclosure requirements the responsibility of the social media platforms themselves. They should not only have an incentive to do so, but could perform the role most efficiently. Most importantly, the government would then not be in a position of directly monitoring or censoring American social media activity.

Respectfully submitted by Sean Kanuck, Director for Future Conflict and Cyber Security, IISS-Americas.

---

[1] *See e.g.,* https://www.theguardian.com/technology/2017/nov/19/trump-russia-fake-news-libertarians-autocrats-democracy

[2] http://www.mid.ru/en/foreign_policy/official_documents/-/asset_publisher/CptICkB6BZ29/content/id/2563163

[3] *See* THE TRANSFORMATION OF RUSSIA'S ARMED FORCES: TWENTY LOST YEARS, edited by Roger N. McDermott (2016), page 205.

[4] https://www.dni.gov/files/documents/ICA_2017_01.pdf

[5] See https://www.dni.gov/files/documents/ICA_2017_01.pdf

[6] *See e.g.,* https://www.nytimes.com/2017/10/01/technology/facebook-russia-ads.html

[7] *See e.g.,* https://www.nytimes.com/2017/09/27/technology/twitter-russia-election.html

[8] *See* https://www.npr.org/2017/10/20/559113223/russian-magazine-says-trolls-used-social-media-to-disrupt-u-s-election

[9] *See* https://www.washingtonpost.com/politics/facebook-says-it-sold-political-ads-to-russian-company-during-2016-election/2017/09/06/32f01fd2-931e-11e7-89fa-bb822a46da5b_story.html?utm_term=.164469bf21d8

[10] *See e.g.,* http://www.chicagotribune.com/news/opinion/commentary/ct-russia-facebook-ads-20171102-story.html

[11] *See e.g.,* https://www.loc.gov/law/help/campaign-finance-regulation/unitedkingdom.php

[12] *See e.g.,* https://www.defcon.org/images/defcon-25/DEF%20CON%2025%20voting%20village%20report.pdf

[13] *See e.g.,* https://www.wired.com/2016/08/twitter-says-suspended-360000-suspected-terrorist-accounts-year/

Appendix II

ADDITIONAL MATERIAL FOR THE RECORD

Cybersecurity for the Real World™

October 24, 2017

Congressman Clay Higgins
Louisiana 3rd District Representative
Member, SST Oversight Subcommittee

Congressman Higgins,

I am writing to express my appreciation for the action being consider to protect our national security interests by limiting or eliminating the use of foreign information technology security software. I am offering my professional insight and expert opinion to impress upon you the necessity of the immediacy of that action. There is a common misconception of how security software functions and the ultimate level of vulnerability that must be allowed for security software to function. I believe, if this vulnerability is revealed, our country will take immediate action to bolster our defenses and secure our assets.

Historically, in my experience, The United States has an established defensive posture regarding foreign super powers and espionage. The purpose of that posture has been to protect national interests from potential espionage efforts. The technology has dramatically shifted from remote listening telemetry to modern Cyberwar – espionage no longer requires physical presence, the worldwide network of connected infrastructure and data and systems provides a remote platform for gathering and transferring stolen information. Cyber technology has enabled an entirely new form of threats and not just from government agencies, now unscrupulous actors engage in data theft and ransomware. Some for political stature and others for financial gains.

Many security software users believe that security software is akin to a shield or a knight's armor. That this shield wards off would be attackers. The reality is that security software is more similar to an inoculation. Security software resides deep inside the computers and infrastructure within the very most sensitive and secure areas. In order to install any effective security software, we must first expose the system making all information vulnerable. The security software has full access to all input/output operations. Security software is fully embedded in such a way that it has complete and total system access. Therefore, it is of the utmost importance that we fully trust in these security applications and understand the laws they are governed by. So why would we expose and make our systems so vulnerable to any foreign super power? Kaspersky is security software, when installed all information accessed by or residing on the system is available to the software. Kaspersky is governed by the laws of the Russian Federation. Reflecting on my career in my military and post-active duty, we sure would have loved to walk right into Moscow and insert our surveillance systems right in the Kremlin!

Make no mistake, the potential security risks of allowing any foreign governed security software onto any system poses a significant risk! I do not wish to cast any negative remarks towards Kaspersky Lab's security software. In fact, their team contributed to catching the famed Karbanak gang, which was responsible for billions of dollars of bank fraud. However, I simply cannot understand why anyone would even consider taking

the risk of inviting foreign governed security software into the very core of our own federal government infrastructure. Assuming that Kaspersky has been cast out of the federal technology systems, we must now identify the best process to not only uninstall, but to completely remediate any risk of compromise and ensure the security and integrity of the systems. We must be able to ensure the CIA (Confidentiality, Integrity, and Availability) triad is intact.

I recommend these actions. Address the complete removal of all foreign security software from all federal systems. Recommend to the business world that foreign security software be avoided for the preservation of proprietary data. Leverage the NIST Cybersecurity Framework and Managed Cybersecurity Service Providers. Engage with MSP's proficient in the space and with certifications and clearances to meet the highest security requirements. Hardware and software must meet WISP and functional requirements while offering elasticity and complete audit controls. Develop and select products in line with NIST Cybersecurity framework. Leverage Secure cloud services, such as Microsoft Azure and Amazon Web. Train all staff with WISP (Written Information Security Program and Policies). Assess and Audit systems and staff to ensure adherence to WISP.

Let's get this tight sir.

I will make myself available to the committee as needed to explore these ideas further.

Best regards.

Troy A. Newman, CISSP

Cyber5

18 Augusta Pines Drive, Suite 150, Spring TX 77389

Troy@cyber5.com | http://www.cyber5.com

Tel:+1713.982.8004 - Office | Tel:+1281.236.4598 - Mobile

Top Reasons to raise concern regarding Kaspersky Security Software -

- EULA (End User License Agreement) - Governed by the laws of the Russian Federation.
- EULA (End User License Agreement) - Software components that use geolocation, the camera or GPS functions...
- Close association with high ranking officials in FSB, KGB, Russian Govt. - socializing regularly in "Banyagate"
- Close ties to Russian Govt - educated at KGB-sponsored cryptography institute, and worked with Russian military intelligence. " A Specialist in Cryptography from KGB".
- Quick command of FSB and Russian Police to recover kidnapped son (in a country that seems unphased by regular kidnappings)
- Supported FSB raids on suspected cybergangs - then employee suddenly imprisoned on accusations of treason
- Certification issues to Kaspersky by Russian Secret Service with military intelligence unit number matching that of FSB program
- Nato Cyber expert quoted " A worldwide deployment of sensors may be too great a temptation for any country's intelligence services to ignore".
- Senate hearing - six high ranking American officials (CIA, FBI, NSA) said under no circumstances would they use Kaspersky software.
- Is it coincidence that the DNC acquired Kaspersky security software in August of 2016; and then had a multitude of information leaks? (Federal Election Commission records show the purchase).
- New VPN product that requires access to all phone data in order to use it? Where are the servers? Are they logging and mining all traffic?
- Timing of New Free Products just becoming available.
- Why should we take the risk knowing the affiliations and understanding the deep access security software has to our systems? There are several US based security products that many consider superior!

10/25/2017

Kaspersky: We uploaded US documents but quickly deleted them

Kaspersky: We uploaded US documents but quickly deleted them

By RAPHAEL SATTER
Today

https://ww

RELATED TOPICS

Anti-virus software
Technology
Business
United States
Europe
Russia
Software

More from
International News

PARIS (AP) — Sometime in 2014, a group of analysts walked into the office of Eugene Kaspersky, the ebullient founder of Russian cybersecurity firm Kaspersky Lab, to deliver some sobering news.

Kaspersky's anti-virus software had automatically scraped powerful digital surveillance tools off a computer in the United States and the analysts were worried: The data's headers clearly identified the files as classified.

"They immediately came to my office," Kaspersky recalled, "and they told me that they have a problem."

He said there was no hesitation about what to do with the cache.

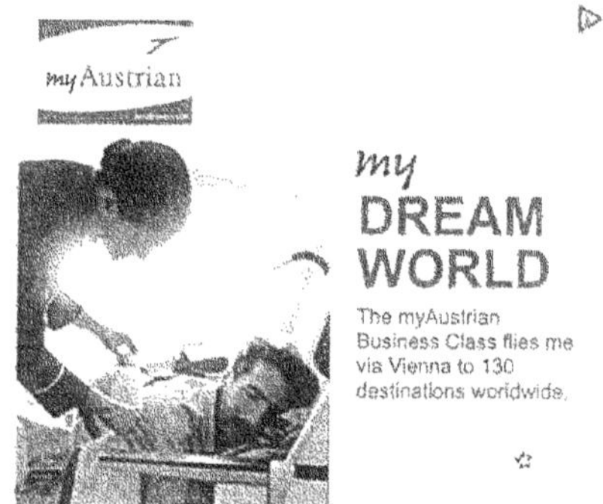

"It must be deleted," Kaspersky says he told them.

The incident, recounted by Kaspersky during a brief telephone interview on Tuesday and supplemented by a timeline and other information provided by company officials, could not immediately be corroborated. But it's the first public acknowledgement of a story that has been building for the past three weeks — that Kaspersky's popular anti-virus program uploaded powerful digital espionage tools belonging to the National Security Agency from a computer in the United States and sent them to servers in Moscow.

The account provides new perspective on the U.S. government's recent move to blacklist Kaspersky from federal computer networks, even if it still leaves important questions unanswered.

To hear Kaspersky tell it, the incident was an accident borne of carelessness.

Analysts at his company were already on the trail of the Equation Group — a powerful group of hackers later exposed as an arm of the NSA — when a computer in the United States was flagged for further investigation. The machine's owner, identified in media reports as an NSA worker, had run anti-virus scans on their home computer after it was infected by a pirated copy of Microsoft Office, according to a Kaspersky timeline released Wednesday.

Kaspersky: We uploaded US documents but quickly deleted them

The scan didn't just treat the infection. It also triggered an alert for Equation Group files the worker had left in a compressed archive which was then spirited to Moscow for analysis.

Kaspersky's story at least partially matches accounts published in The New York Times, The Washington Post and The Wall Street Journal. All three publications recently reported that someone at the NSA's elite hacking unit lost control of some of the agency's powerful surveillance tools after they brought their work home with them, leaving what should have been closely guarded code on a personal computer running Kaspersky's anti-virus software.

But information security experts puzzling over the hints dropped by anonymous government officials are still wondering at whether Kaspersky is suspected of deliberately hunting for confidential data or was merely doing its job by sniffing out suspicious files.

Much of the ambiguity is down to the nature of modern anti-virus software, which routinely submits rogue files back to company servers for analysis. The software can easily be quietly tweaked to scoop up other files, too: perhaps classified documents belonging to a foreign rival's government, for example.

Concerns have been fanned by increasingly explicit warnings from U.S. government officials after tensions with Russia escalated in the wake of the 2016 presidential election.

Kaspersky denies any inappropriate link to the Russian government, and said in his interview that any classified documents inadvertently swept up by his software would be destroyed on discovery.

"If we see confidential or classified information, it will be immediately deleted and that was exactly (what happened in) this case," he said, adding that the order had since been written into company policy.

An AP request for a copy of that policy wasn't immediately granted.

Kaspersky's account still has some gaps. For example, why not alert American authorities to what happened? The newspaper reports alleged that the U.S. learned that Kaspersky had acquired the NSA's tools via an Israeli spying operation.

Kaspersky declined to say whether he had ever alerted U.S. authorities to the incident.

"Do you really think that I want to see in the news that I tried to contact the NSA to report this case?" he said at one point. "Definitely I don't want to see that in the news."

So did he alert the NSA to the incident or not?

"I'm afraid I can't answer the question," he said.

Even if some questions linger, Kaspersky's explanation sounds plausible, said Jake Williams, a former NSA analyst and the founder of Augusta, Georgia-based Rendition InfoSec. He noted that Kaspersky was pitching itself at the time to government clients in the United States and may not have wanted the risk of having classified documents on its network.

"It makes sense that they pulled those up and looked at the classification marking and then deleted them," said Williams. "I can see where it's so toxic you may not want it on your systems."

As for the insinuation that someone at the NSA not only walked highly classified software out of the building but put it on a computer running a bootleg version of Office, Williams called it "absolutely wild."

"It's hard to imagine a worse PR nightmare for the NSA," he said.

———

Online:

Kaspersky's timeline:

https://www.kaspersky.com/blog/internal-investigation-preliminary-results/19894/

More From AP

by Taboola

Authorities: Bodies in California desert locked in embrace

US astronaut's memoir provides blunt take on year in space

Mike Ditka apologizes for comment on racial oppression

Man admits fatally shooting daughter over lack of 'respect'

Ad Content

9 781985 626126